D0521968
Black Sea
Crimea
Sevastopol
Hungary
Bulgaria
Roumelia
Greece
ATHENS
CONSTANTINOPLE
Chan. of Constantinople
Adrianople
Salonika
Asia Minor
Smyrna
Angora
Rhodes
Cyprus
Candia
G. of Adalia
Mediterranean Sea
G. of Sidra
Barca
Alexandria
CAIRO
Oasis of Siwah
Libyan Desert
G. of Suez
Egypt
Nile
Telegraph

THE VANADIS

1880

SUNRISE ON THE MEDITERRANEAN

2002

First published in the United States of America in 2004
by Rizzoli International Publications, Inc.,
300 Park Avenue South, New York, NY 10010
www.rizzoliusa.com

2004 2005 2006 2007/ 10 9 8 7 6 5 4 3 2 1
Distributed in the U.S. trade by St. Martin's Press, New York
Printed in China
ISBN: 0-8478-2609-0

Library of Congress Cataloging-in-Publication Data
Wharton, Edith, 1862-1937.
The cruise of the Vanadis / Edith Wharton;
photographs by Jonas
Dovydenas.— 1st American ed.
p. cm.
ISBN 0-8478-2609-0
1. Mediterranean Region—Description and travel.
2. Wharton, Edith, 1862-1937—Travel—Mediterranean Region.
3. Americans—Mediterranean Region—History.
4. Vanadis (Frigate) I. Dovydenas, Jonas. II. Title.
D973.W56 2004
910'.9163'809034—dc22
2003025705

William R. Tyler has waived the royalties
from this book as a gift
to Edith Wharton Restoration.

Contents

FOR THEIR GENEROUS ASSISTANCE,
RIZZOLI AND EDITH WHARTON RESTORATION
WISH TO THANK:

Claudine Lesage who found and identified the tapuscript,
Françoise Gattegno and the Municipal Library in Hyères who kept it,
Anne Luyat for kind advice,
Jacques Darras who contributed to the first publishing effort,
The Watkins Loomis Agency,
and William R. Tyler.

Foreword

by

Louis Auchincloss

2003

Edith Wharton in her memoirs, *A Backward Glance*, relates how in the winter of 1888, then a bride of three years, aged twenty-six, she confided in a Newport friend and cousin-in-law, James Van Alen, that she would give anything in the world to make a cruise in the Mediterranean. But she was not prepared for his answer: "You needn't do that if you'd let me charter a yacht and come with me."

Van Alen meant what he said. He was a hearty and adventurous soul, a world traveler, a member of an old Knickerbocker family and the widower of Edith's second cousin, Emily Astor who had died in childbirth. He had volunteered to fight the Turks in Greece in Lord Mulcaster's ill-fated expedition in the 1870s, but had fortunately been prevented from going by a last minute attack of malaria. He was rich enough to pay his half of the charter of the yacht *Vanadis*, but Edith and her husband Teddy had to come up with their half, which they sportingly did, though it amounted for them a full year's income. Luck, however was on their side, for a distant cousin of Edith's died while they were at sea, and her unanticipated share of his estate more than covered the cost of a cruise which Edith called a "taste of heaven."

The account that she kept of this excursion is the only writing of hers of which we have any knowledge, except for some juvenilia, from the first quarter century of her life. As a published writer she was certainly a late starter. Keats was dead at an age when she had still not begun. But those earlier years had not been wasted. She not only read deeply in English, French, Italian and German literature; her keen eyes had taken in and her copious memory had recorded the myriad details of her childhood visits to Europe and her home life in brownstone Manhattan and the shingle villas of Newport. She had stored a gallery in her mind from which she would be able to illustrate the many volumes she was destined to write.

The portrait that the French novelist, Paul Burget, provided of a Newport intellectual matron in Outremer (1893) has long been recognized as Edith Wharton. She "has read everything, understood everything, not superficially but really, with an energy of culture that could put to shame the whole Parisian fraternity of letters." And yet he found himself longing to cry, "Oh, for one ignorance, one error, just a single one!" But he longed in vain.

One can see a little of what he means in reading the account of her cruise. Edith Wharton's observations are so richly detailed, so vividly expressed, and, one is sure, with so unerring a taste, and so accurate a rendition, that one wonders at times if any tourist could really be so exquisitely equipped for the experience of travel. Yet any such begrudgment is soon swept away by the excitement of feeling that one is witnessing the genesis of a great literary career. Edith Wharton was not going to subject herself or the public to the spectacle of any awkward first steps; all of these would be kept to herself until she was ready to present a really finished product. The style of her first published work of fiction, "The Greater Inclination" (1890), did not have to be improved upon for the rest of her long literary life. In her log of the *Vanadis* we have a kind of dress rehearsal for the fiction of one of America's greatest novelists.

The diary, if diary it was—and the sharpness of its details certainly suggests an almost daily recording—is strictly limited to just what Edith saw at each Ionian or Aegean stop. One occasionally has a glimpse of the author's sometimes rather domineering personality in her admissions that her rigorous schedule of exhaustive sightseeing may have caused a bit of a strain on her two more easygoing male companions, and we note that she found the captain surly and indifferent. There are also moments when she voices her dissent from popular opinion, as when she suggests that the famous Sicilian cathedral at Monreale lacks depth and variety of color, or when she disagrees with those romantics who find ruins improved by their very dilapidation. How the architect of the temples at Girgenti, she exclaims, would have shuddered to think that "his raw masses of sandstone would remain exposed to the eyes of future critics!"

For the most part, however, the beauties of nature and ancient civilization speak for themselves in her vivid and elegant prose, and the splendid photographs of Jonas Dovydenas of the actual scenes she describes shed a fascinating modern light on a world that has actually changed very little since the cruise of the *Vanadis*—and where it has changed tourists would not be anxious to penetrate. The industries of the day,

Edith states, might be a source of pride to modern Greeks, "but very uninteresting to the traveler who has hoped in sailing eastward to leave the practical realities of life behind."

So minutely does Edith observe the phenomena that attract her that it is hard to believe that she was only a day or two in most of the sites visited. Take for example this description of what the women of Amorgos had on: "They wore linen petticoats grotesquely embroidered with images of beasts and birds in red and green silks, and some had linen jackets, still more elaborately embroidered, with enormously wide sleeves; while others wore skirts and jackets of scarlet cloth. All of them had chemisettes of gold-embroidered gauze and necklaces of old coins; while their heads were wound in long yellow scarves falling to their shoulders."

One can see in the diary the trained eye that would one day enable its possessor to recreate the gleaming overstuffed Victorian interiors of Fifth Avenue and the small bright lawns and big bright sea of Newport, as so unforgettably depicted in *The Age of Innocence*. Edmund Wilson would call Edith Wharton the pioneer and poet of interior decoration, but her gardens were just as fine as her houses, in her books as in her life.

We see in what she wrote about her cruise that she was ready to set her stages, to fill her backgrounds, to create the world in which her characters would enact her plots. The characters and plots would come in due time.

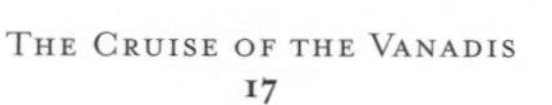

Introduction

by

Claudine Lesage

SAINT-JOSSE-SUR-MER, JUNE 1991

The route which led me to Edith Wharton's manuscript *The Cruise of the* Vanadis was rather a strange one. Although many a major discovery seems to be made by chance or luck, finding Edith Wharton's lost manuscript had very little to do with either. It was rather the result of a painstaking task, which had occupied me for many years, but one which had no connection at all with Edith Wharton. And if I had not lived for a few weeks in Hyères on the Avenue Edith Wharton, I would never have been attracted by the leather bound but unsigned pages that were shown to me at the Municipal Library there.

At the time, my subject of research was Joseph Conrad. The Avenue Edith Wharton runs above the boarding house that Polish friends of Conrad's had owned and where he had, most presumably, stayed when he first came to the Mediterranean. When, as was often the case, I chose to walk down a flight of stairs from the Avenue Edith Wharton, I arrived directly in front of Conrad's former lodgings; when I chose to go up the stairs, I arrived in what had been Edith Wharton's gardens—now turned into a city park—where I had access to the terrace in front of the Villa Sainte Claire.

The terrace and the gardens were pleasant, but what fascinated me was the view from the heights where it is located. It seemed, as I overlooked the Golden Isles and the Bay of Hyères,micah that I had before me the seascape of the last chapter of *The Rover.* Because I was concentrating on Conrad's novels, I was not fully conscious that I had been living all the while in the specific atmosphere that had been Edith Wharton's during her life in France. Going to that garden meant talking to the gardeners, learning the name of such and such a rose or thinking as I walked along the paths: "This must have been where the greenhouse was . . . and what about the empty shaded paths?" One felt that the owner of the place had left for a time but certainly not forever.

Nevertheless, my work on Joseph Conrad was progressing fairly well. I had been discussing the subject with Françoise Gattegno, the librarian in Hyères, when she suddenly disappeared behind a bookcase saying: "Oh, I wanted to show you something . . . we have had it for some time, I don't know how long, I don't know where it comes from or how we got it either . . . Here it is, typed in English. . . ."

I had no idea whatsoever of what it might be but the minute I opened it, I knew it was something exceptional. I read a few lines about a garden in Algiers, saw the ex-libris, closed it and gave it back. Being so much engrossed in my search on Conrad, I might have forgotten the entire occurrence if it had not been for that description of that garden in Algiers, and of street-scenes such as this one: "Nowhere in Europe could one see anything so Oriental as the little arcaded café at Mustapha, where robed Algerines sit crouched on the terrace, drinking their coffee under a group of plane trees. We passed the summer palace of the Governor, getting a glimpse of well-kept gardens through the gateways . . ." In Hyères, had I not had similar glimpses through gateways into very private gardens, into writers' secret gardens?

My investigation into Conrad's past was coming to an end. I had come to the conclusion that, in the house down the hill, he had lived some strange and dramatic love story which was to become later the essence, the very core of his work as a writer. I cannot say that I had been unconscious of Edith Wharton during that time, that wouldn't be true. I knew she had been in the background all the while but I didn't know yet how she was to fit into the completed landscape. That is the reason why I left the manuscript untouched for two more years, left it lying on a remote bookshelf in an obscure corner of the library. It had been sleeping there for more than fifty years, would one or two extra years make a notable difference?

When, at last, I took the time to read it closely, I experienced that intoxicating feeling of being the only person, except the author, to have read those pages. I cherished the strange circumstances which had given me such a privilege; I now know how a miser would feel when contemplating his cassette, I now understand why an art collector sometimes keeps his paintings for himself, hidden away from the rest of the world.

The euphoria was followed by the sudden realization that many questions remained unanswered. Why was it that Edith Wharton had never published the manuscript? Did it deal with matters too personal to be brought to the knowledge of the public? Did Edith Wharton feel that such an early try was not worth publishing? May it simply be that she never intended, while writing, to publish her account of the voyage? Is it possible to assume that everything written afterwards was composed with publication in mind? Whatever the answers to these questions may be, we do know that she never used the material from the *Vanadis* cruise in any of her fictional works, with the possible exception of the heroine of *The House of Mirth* going on a vague cruise in the Mediterranean. Whereas Conrad in similar circumstances would have written five hundred pages on the subject, changing the biographical material into fiction, Edith Wharton erases it entirely from her published writing.

Other questions followed in the wake of the first ones, the most improbable making me doubt at times whether Edith Wharton herself had done the writing. Strangely enough, it was the manuscript itself which, like a stubborn piece of evidence, gave me the assurance I needed. Her style is unmistakable even in this first effort. Having ". . . a moderately good breakfast in a not over clean dining-room . . ." is a mean and depreciative remark that some Mrs. Dagonet or Marvell (*The House of Mirth*) would actually have said in similar circumstances. Once I had identified her style, I asked myself another question: Could this manuscript possibly be a diary written in 1926 when she made a second trip to the Aegean Islands? The date which is watermarked on the paper (1896) is no real obstacle, but she had sailed on that occasion on board the *Osprey* and not the *Vanadis* . . . One must add that though the manuscript contains many details concerning days, months and dates, information concerning the year is entirely lacking. There is only one datable piece: that year, Easter was on Sunday, April 1st and, if such was the case, then, the only year possible would have been 1888, a fact which her biographer, Richard Lewis, confirms[1]:

> One day in the winter of 1888, Edith exclaimed to a friend that she would give everything she owned to make a cruise through the Aegean islands. The friend, James Van

1. Lewis, Richard. *Edith Wharton, A Biography*. Harper & Row, 1975

Alen (scion of one of the very good old New-York families), replied that such a cruise need not cost as much as all that, and that he would be happy to charter a yacht if the Whartons would come as his guests. Edith and Teddy, appreciative as they were decided it would be a better arrangement if they divided the expenses with Van Alen, and so feel free to make suggestions about some of the ports of call. Upon calculation, it turned out that their share of the four-month trip would almost exactly equal their total income for an entire year: about ten thousand dollars. Edith's brothers, the co-executors of her trust fund, remonstrated strongly; the entire Wharton clan protested that a cruise of this kind was unheard of and preposterous. Edith wavered, but when Teddy asked her if she seriously wanted to go and she made it clear that she did, he simply said "Come along, then."

So, that was it! She had most certainly kept some diary during her first cruise to the Mediterranean, had it typed by a secretary some years later, had it bound but never had it published. Her pleasure was to read it, sitting on the white terrace overlooking the tiers of red tiled roofs down toward the blue bay of Hyères and the even bluer lagoon of Pesquiers.

Knowing precisely what Edith Wharton had done during the end of winter and the beginning of spring 1888 is not a matter of little interest but there is an undercurrent which is even more fascinating since it is one of the first texts of some length she ever wrote apart from the fragments of poetry which she had tried beforehand and a miscarried attempt at a novel entitled *Fast and Loose* in 1876. And though it has often been thought that her beginnings as a writer were a mere accident, an occupation for an idle rich woman, *The Cruise of the* Vanadis tends to prove the contrary. Just as a violonist diligently practises her scales before appearing in front of an audience, she had been writing extensively though privately.

It is also possible to assume that she wrote the completed manuscript from notes once she had returned home. These pages nevertheless form a most unusual corpus for a young woman's diary. Paradoxically what matters most is not what she says or even alludes to but what is obviously missing. And, as if to counterbalance what she did not wish to reveal she accumulates historical details and descriptions, using for this purpose her diary as if it was a camera and taking photos of the most striking views she encounters.

It would seem that she had already discovered the technique which would eventually become the hallmark of her style: the art of omission. She never indicates who her two companions—her husband, Teddy Wharton, and James Van Alen—may be and she uses the singular and plural first-person pronouns interchangeably. On one precise occasion, she is obliged to use "they" standing for her two fellow-travellers as they visit Mount Athos without her because the monasteries were closed to women. She nevertheless writes her description just as if she too had been able to see it with her own eyes.

Did she then realize that something was lacking, that she was definitely omitting too much, that until then she had been reacting passively—a kind of blank and neutral darkroom, a photographic lens which simply recorded the image presented to it? She was intensely aware that Mount Athos was their farthest point of navigation in the Aegean Sea, that the return voyage awaited her, and the moment she had anticipated for so long was to be denied her because of her sex: "the early established rule of no female, human or animal, is to set foot on the promontory, is maintained as strictly as ever," she wrote. The frustration was such that after a detailed description of a place she never actually saw, her imagination began responding more actively. From that point on in the manuscript, her style comes to life as does her sense of humour as she portrays the caloyers, "with their shocks of black hair and long woollen robes flying behind them . . . a wild enough looking set to frighten any intruder away, as they clambered hurriedly down the hill to prevent my landing." Her writing becomes more precise and finds images such as the one she uses to describe the columns of Jupiter Olympius in Athens which stood "picturesquely clustered among their fallen fellows." Her short but lively accounts of nautical difficulties when arriving in Italy show her mastery of both tone and technique.

This diary has literary ambition and, in a way, achieves it. One can be sure that she had read Goethe's *Travels in Italy* but had she read Flaubert's *Voyage En Orient*? Her references seem to be earlier and sound more romantic, more purely descriptive and her style makes one think of painting—of Orientalist painters like Decamps—rather than of literature. Moreover, if the first scenes captured by her camera diary tend to look like stiff postcards or even awkward watercolours, one gets the feeling that she is already learning to master her instrument and, as she turns back to Italy, she has definitely become a full-grown writer and the metamorphosis is complete.

Whatever Edith Wharton's reasons were for not having this text published, I finally came to the conclusion that the responsibility was no longer hers but mine. In the course of literary research, it is indeed an obligation to reveal discoveries which will aid others in their understanding of great writers and their works. Moreover it seems to me that Edith Wharton would not feel distressed if we decided to accompany her on a voyage which she described many years later as "the crowning wonder of my life," to accompany her on her maiden "Odyssey" into literature.

A Note about the Photographs

by

Jonas Dovydenas

Lenox, Massachusetts, 2003

Edith Wharton spent eighty-two days sailing aboard the *Vanadis*. I confess I had neither the inner nor the outer resources to do what she did. What I did do was travel for three weeks each spring for three years. First I went to Africa, Malta, and Sicily, then I made two trips to the Greek Islands. But what I lost in continuity I gained in time to savor the riches I encountered in following Edith Wharton's footsteps.

I was astonished by her pace. Clearly, lingering was not her style. Only high seas or a bad cold kept her from charging ahead. *The Cruise of the* Vanadis is not a story of leisurely on-board meals in exotic places; this is a look at the Mediterranean world through the eyes of a young woman whose mind was everywhere, always full sail ahead into territory she had studied and prepared for. She knew how to look and find and judge—always judge. (If you are not interested in opinions, don't come near Edith Wharton.)

She was most passionate about going to see for herself. The luxury of a yacht well-crewed and provisioned did not excite her, or if it did, she does not mention it. She mentions Teddy, her husband of three years, and James Van Alen, only as "fellow travelers." In her journal, she pays attention to the journey only.

Much of what she saw has been worn away by human activity, or jumbled by earthquakes and wars. Don't look for the mixture of "Orientalism and European civilization" she encountered in Smyrna—it's gone. A modern and dull Izmir has replaced it. Yet, what remains today exactly as she saw it in 1888 is as astonishing and mysterious as the light in the Cathedral in Syracuse, the house of worship that began as a temple to Athena some twenty-five centuries ago.

My intent in taking these photographs was not just to find places she visited, but to be right where she might have stood and looked around. I am accustomed to interpret my assignments freely, but here I had to look at things through her eyes, if I could. Edith Wharton sought order and harmony and she expressed her thoughts in prose as deliberately worked as carved marble. I had to honor that.

The stones she saw will survive the next hundred years as easily as they survived the centuries before her visit. The Temple of Concord in Agrigento (Girgenti) still stands above a grove of olive trees; the glory of the Pallatine Chapel in Palermo is exactly as she saw it in 1888; the streets of Corfu have changed hardly at all, nor has the color of the marble of the Parthenon. Moreover, many of the places she visited are today almost free of the accretions that grow so prolifically anyplace where there is a stream of tourists. Finally, since many of the ruins have not been restored, they are much the same as they were when Edith Wharton visited them.

I found other, more subtle pleasures. The festival of the Annunciation on the island of Tinos was celebrated exactly as she described it. On Rhodes, I came across a small stable of donkeys in Lindos town—surely they must be the descendants of the donkeys that carried her in her wide saddle. On a road above Mytilene, I came across a trickle of water by the side of the road, "a stream fringed with oleanders." This seemed to me a greater miracle than the endurance of the Roman aqueduct several hundred yards away, which she also mentions. The shrines on the walls of houses in Palermo no longer have candles, but little electric lights illuminate the Sicilian heart just the same. The old world survives its contact with the new world. Indeed, I feel that signs of our times add new dimensions to and emphasize the enduring accuracy of Edith Wharton's observations.

I chose sites that were the most accessible to me and to the ordinary traveler. I have some regret I did not visit every place that the *Vanadis* did, but for a number of reasons that was not possible.

Edith Wharton was good company to me and my travelling companion, my wife, Betsy. Her precise observations and opinions were always refreshing. She focused our attention on what was truly important when we might have easily been distracted. Reading her sentences over and over, looking for a match, was a pleasure in itself.

Following Edith Wharton's footsteps would not have been possible without travel agents, hotel guidebooks, or flight information off the Internet, but had I travelled without *The Cruise of the* Vanadis in my camera bag, I would have been merely wandering.

THE MOUNT AND EDITH WHARTON RESTORATION

Edith Wharton designed and built her country estate, The Mount, in 1902. Located in Lenox, Massachusetts, it is one of only five percent of National Historic Landmarks dedicated to women. In addition to being one of America's greatest novelists, Wharton's influence on American residential architecture, landscape design and interior design is substantial, and The Mount is the only full expression of her design principles. During her decade of residence at The Mount, Wharton produced some of her most important literary works, including *The House of Mirth* and *Ethan Frome*.

Edith Wharton Restoration was founded in 1980 to preserve and restore The Mount as a tribute to its remarkable creator and to establish it as a center for celebrating the literary arts and recognizing women of achievement. A significant portion of the house and formal gardens have been restored. The Mount is open to the public daily. For more information, please visit: www.EdithWharton.org.

Wär nur ein Zaubermantel mein
Und trüg er mich in fremde Länder
Mir sollt'er um die köstlichsten Gewänder,
Nicht feil um einen Königsmantel sein.

Yea! If only a magic coat were mine,
To carry me to places strange,
Not for costly treasures would I exchange,
Not for a king's coat fine.

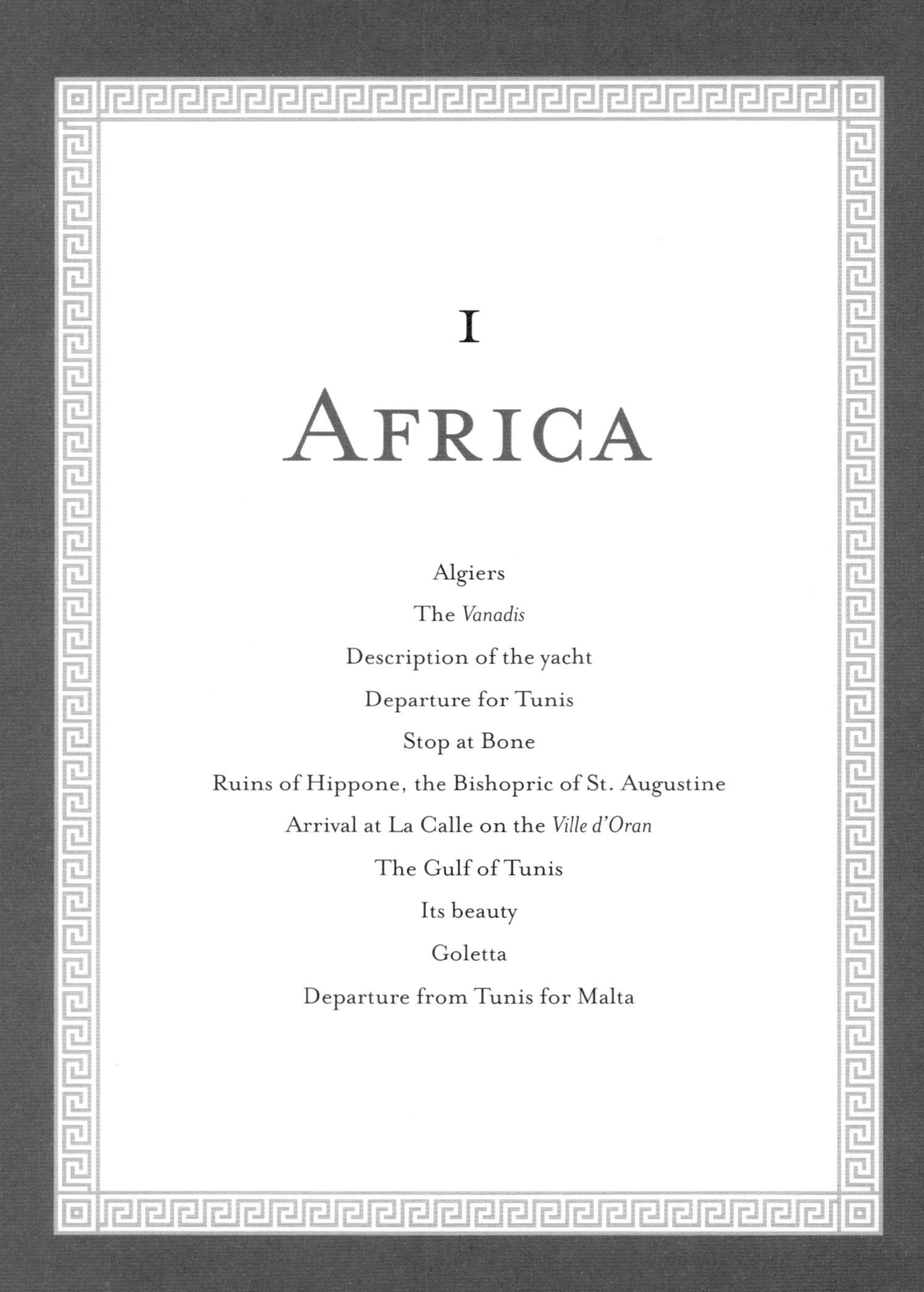

I

Africa

Algiers

The *Vanadis*

Description of the yacht

Departure for Tunis

Stop at Bone

Ruins of Hippone, the Bishopric of St. Augustine

Arrival at La Calle on the *Ville d'Oran*

The Gulf of Tunis

Its beauty

Goletta

Departure from Tunis for Malta

On the seventeenth of February after two weeks of icy fog in Paris, we left Marseilles for Algiers, in the steamer *Ville de Madrid*. The Gulf of Lions was in its usual disturbed condition, and it was after a very rough passage that we reached Algiers on the following night. The steam-yacht *Vanadis*, which we had chartered in England for our Mediterranean cruise, lay awaiting us in the harbour, and the gig came alongside the steamer as soon as we anchored.

We had to row ashore first, to pass through the Custom House, in common with all the other passengers; and on setting foot in the sea of mud which covered the landing-place, we were surrounded by the first Arabs we had ever seen—startlingly picturesque in the flashes of lantern-light, with their white burnouses and long white cloaks. A few minutes later we were again in the gig, being rapidly rowed across the wide harbour, under a sky glittering with stars, and our first view of Algiers, stretching its illuminated curve high above the dark waters of the bay, was extremely fine. We were soon alongside the yacht, and presently found ourselves peacefully seated at supper in the brightly lighted saloon, which had been filled with roses and violets in honour of our coming.

As soon as we had supped, we proceeded to inspect our yacht, little thinking, as we found our way from one room to another, with what a home-like feeling she would soon be invested. The *Vanadis* is a steam-yacht of 333 tons, with a length of 167 feet over all, and 21 feet beam. On deck there is a comfortable deck-house, with seats along the sides, a table, and racks over-head. Below there is a large saloon, plainly paneled in maple, with two long swinging tables, a small stove, and a shelf for books running the whole length of both sides of the saloon, above the sofas. One of the two tables we used to dine at, the other was soon covered with a varied collection of inkstands, blotting-books, maps and vases of flowers. Aft of the saloon were our two state-rooms, occupying the full width of the yacht, and comfortably fitted with shelves, drawers, hanging-closets and large bath-tubs. Foreward were our fellow-traveller's room, two rooms for the maid and valet, and a fourth in which they took their meals. The engines and the men's quarters were of course aft. The crew numbered sixteen, and consisted of the captain and mate, two engineers, two firemen, the boatswain, five able seamen, two stewards and two cooks.

We spent three days and a half in Algiers, but as I was ill and passed the greater part of my time on the yacht, my recollections of it are much less clear than of many other places where we only stayed for a few hours. Never was town more nobly placed. Backed by the green slopes of the Sahel, the tiers of white houses follow the long curve of the bay, above which they are raised by the high arches of the terrace-like Boulevard de la République, and over the denser roofs of the city lie the scattered villas of Mustapha Supérieur, their horse-shoe windows glancing seaward through groves of orange and palm, their white walls tapestried with crimson bougainvillea. The harbour, crowded with shipping, is bounded on one side by a mole of modern construction, on the other by the jetty which thirty thousand Christian captives toiled to build less than four hundred years ago. But the reality of Christian slavery in Africa is brought much closer to us by Goethe's description of Prince Palagonia whom he saw, hardly more than a hundred years ago, clad in black small-clothes, with silk stockings and silver buckles, begging in the streets of Palermo for money to ransom the Christian captives of Algeria. Even in 1816 three thousand still remained to be released by Lord Exmouth when he destroyed the fleet of the Algerine pirates.

It seems incredible that such things should have been within the memory of living man, when one walks today through the street of the French quarter, crowded with carriages and tourists, and lined with shops as inviting as those of Nice.

To see the Arab side of Algiers one must go to the market or the mosques, or better still, climb the steep lanes which lead upward from the Parisian arcades of the Rue Bab-Azoun. In these narrow streets, we saw veiled women hurrying along with the peculiar shuffling gait due to those loose slippers of the East, their painted eyes shining through the thin white yashmak; then there were dark doorways in which old Arabs sat squatting over their tailoring or shoe-making; and groups of stalking Bedouins in ragged garments which had once been white, and negroes and Jews and half-clothed children, and all the other fantastic figures which go to make up the pageantry of an Eastern street scene. We hired a little phaeton one day, and drove out to Mustapha Supérieur, catching charming glimpses of walled gardens and Mauresque villas, and meeting omnibuses crowded with wild-looking figures, and driven at a headlong pace down the muddy suburban roads. Mustapha, though quite as pretty as any of the suburbs near Cannes or Nice, lacks the neatness and garden-like look which we associate with the Riviera; but perhaps the general air of slovenliness is atoned for, to many eyes, by the picturesque populace filling the untidy streets. And nowhere in Europe could one see anything so Oriental as the little arcaded café at Mustapha, where white-robed Algerines sit crouched on the terrace, drinking their coffee under a group of plane-trees. We passed the summer palace of the Governor, getting a glimpse of well-kept gardens through the gateways, and then drove through the *Vallon de la Femme Sauvage*. . . .This wild little ravine led us to the quarter called Mustapha Inférieur, lying near the sea on the lower slope of the Sahel; and here we found the Jardin d'Essai, which I was particularly anxious to see. We walked under avenues of India-rubber trees as large as oaks, and between trellises of tea-roses in bloom, and high clumps of Arundo donax, but a cold wind sweeping through the long alleys made the scene cheerless in spite of this southern vegetation. It was, however, a bad time to visit the Jardin d'Essai, for it had been very cold for some days in Europe, and we heard afterwards that there was snow at Avignon and skating near Marseilles, while we were shivering under the India-rubber trees of Algiers. Perhaps it may have been owing to the exceptional weather that all the more delicate palms such as Lantana borbonica, Phoenix, Cycas revoluta, &c, were sheltered by tents of matting.

On the 22d of February, at about 3 p.m., we started for Tunis, but the wind was so high and the sea so rough, that on the following afternoon we put in at Bone. Never was tranquil harbour more welcome, and as soon as we could get pratique we were set ashore and took a walk through the town. It is charmingly situated on a bay surrounded by mountains, and close by lie the ruins of Hippone, the Bishopric of St. Augustine. The town itself is clean and pretty, with an arcaded French quarter, as usual, and a square planted with palms, and beds of roses and violets. At the head of this square stands the modern Catholic cathedral, and a little further on a gate in the wall of the town leads into the country. In the Arab quarter we saw many striking figures—children in bright frocks, with broad gold bracelets, women in white burnouses, with black silk yashmaks over their faces, and strangest of all, the Jewesses with silk turbans over their plaited hair (like 17th century pictures of Judith or Herodias), loose flowing sleeves of embroidered gauze or muslin, and flowered silk dresses with jackets braided with gold.

The afternoon of our arrival we went ashore in the steam-launch, and drove to Hippone. The road lies through a lane overshadowed by high hedges of prickly pear and aloes, behind which we caught glimpses of orange and lemon groves full of fruit. The ruins stand on a hill overgrown with olives and consist of the piers and vaulting of a very old church, covered with a climbing mass of green. Whether it is the church destroyed in the 7th century or a later one, I do not know. Higher up the hill, Catholic ardour is raising the walls and columns of a new Cathedral, the crypt of which is already finished and used as a church. Here we met some Sisters of Charity, who showed us the French Orphanage nearby, and after lingering for some time to look at the beautiful view of mountains, plain and sea, we drove back to Bone. This time our road led through the valley behind the town, skirting a stream overhung with cactuses and blooming mimosa. All the trees were in full leaf, and the land was a blaze of young spring green.

I was still so unwell that on February 24th we decided to take the large steamer *Ville d'Oran* to Malta, stopping at Tunis on the way, while the yacht went straight to Malta as Tunis roadstead is a very bad place to lie in. Of course, no sooner had we decided on this plan, than the wind fell, and we steamed out over a calm sea, followed by the *Vanadis*, and deeply regretting that we had left her. As it turned out, however, I had a lucky escape, for she met bad weather in the Malta channel; and besides we should have been very sorry not to see Tunis. The afternoon was overcast, but the clouds broke away and when we reached the village of La Calle at 7 in the evening the moon shone out over the smooth sea and the fantastic outline of the African mountains. We lay some time at La Calle, a coral-fishing village principally populated by Italians, and the evening was so warm that we sat on deck until late, watching the unloading of a cargo of rails which were to go towards the building of a projected railway, and listening to the strange outbursts of Italian patois from the boats which swarmed about our sides.

The next morning we awoke in the Gulf of Tunis, and I never looked out on a lovelier sight than when I went on deck. To our left lay a clump of mountains ethereal as Shelley's "peaked isles;" to our right, across the water, the cliff of Cape Carthage, with a white village clinging to its side, and the ruins of Carthage on the bay below; and beyond this again, on the water's edge, the long line of Goletta with its flat roofs and domes, and boats with gaily-coloured lateen sails putting out from its crowded wharves. The company's steam-launch took us off to Goletta, the Piraeus of Tunis, and a short walk through the little town brought us to the railway station. While we waited for the train to start we were much amused by watching the strangely-dressed Tunisian women walking in the streets. They wear short blouses to their hips, and their legs, from their feet up, are tightly wound in bands of white linen. To add to the grotesqueness of their appearance, they wear a kind of horned headdress of gold, bound about the temples with a fold of black silk, and nothing can be conceived more ludicrous than the fat, elderly women thus arrayed, who were walking unconcernedly through the cosmopolitan crowd about the railway station.

Presently the archaic little train started on its leisurely progress, skirting the shores of the "El-Bahira" or Salt Lake to the north-east of Tunis, past marshy flats where Arabs were guarding their sheep and cows, with here and there a flat-roofed villa and a cluster of palms, until we reached Tunis station. The Boulevard de la Marine, provincially French as its name implies, led us in a few minutes from the station to the hotel, where we had a moderately good breakfast in a not over-clean dining-room. A short distance beyond the hotel, the Boulevard ends at the Bab-el-Bahr or sea gate, which leads at once into the Arab quarter. Passing through that arch, one leaves behind in a moment the recent civilization which has created the hotel and the Boulevard de la Marine. If certain parts of Tunis have been greatly changed since it passed under the French protectorate, it is hard to believe that others have been in any way affected by it; for nothing can be conceived more purely Oriental than the Bazaars of Tunis. We plunged at once into a steep street, which proved to be the provision-bazaar or market, and which, like all the others, leads up to the Kasbah (the Citadel) on the hill-top. It was thronged with a brightly-tinted crowd, composed of Arabs, veiled women, Jews in richly embroidered garments, water-carriers, sweet-meats sellers carrying trays of dates and candies on their heads, negroes in gaudy robes, donkeys laden with branches of dates, and a hundred other fanciful figures, multi-coloured as a carnival procession. Soon we reached a roofed bazaar where white-robed Tunisians sat in matted niches making yellow shoes. Each bazaar is dedicated almost entirely to one trade, and in the cobbler's bazaar hundreds of yellow shoes line the walls of the dark little shops, and every cobbler seems to have a pair in hand. Overhead, streaks of sunshine filtered through between the roofing of planks, and here and there a tuft of green foliage stood out against the blue sky, while in the shops all was in cool shadow. Another turn, and we found ourselves in a vaulted bazaar, where the saddlers were embroidering harnesses and bridles in gold and silver thread, or lazy merchants, reclining on carpets, drank their coffee, and watched over their bales of silks and gauzes. But who shall describe the cool, greenish light of this whitewashed tunnel, or the picturesque groups crouched in each doorway, or the doorways themselves, with their twisted fret-work painted in bright colours; not forgetting the occasional glimpse of a vaulted courtyard, with a palm against the sky; the gleaming marble columns of the fore-court of a mosque, on whose steps an Arab kneels in prayer; the veiled women shuffling to and fro, the negroes, the dogs, the donkeys, the coffee-shops where coffee is brewed at a blue and white tiled stove for the group of Tunisians who sit in the doorway around tables inlaid with mother-of-pearl? Hard as it is to write of these things vividly, it is harder still to forget a first sight of the Bazaars of Tunis.

As no Christians are allowed to enter the mosques in the Regency of Tunis, we continued our ramble until we reached the whitewashed

Kasbah on the top of the hill (now turned into a barrack) and then went back to the hotel. We met few Christians in the bazaars, and the step through the Bab-el-Bahr to the Boulevard de la Marine, brought us back to civilization as abruptly as we had left it. We hired a carriage, and drove out to the Bardo, the Bey's Summer Palace. The way leads through a squalid modern suburb, a wilderness of white-washed walls and mud and misery; then out into the country between hedges of prickly pear, along a road which is only enlivened by an occasional procession of camels, or a party of veiled women on donkeys. The scenery about Tunis is flat and uninteresting; and though the fortified exterior of the Bardo is fine, it is hardly worth taking the drive for.

Inside, we were led through one or two tiled courts, with remnants of Moorish work about the doorways, to what the attendant evidently thought the only thing worth showing: a suite of state apartments, furnished in the worst European taste of forty years ago, and adorned with the usual number of clocks with which Eastern potentates love to surround themselves.

We returned to Tunis and took the afternoon train back to Goletta, where we found that the steam-launch had already left the wharf, and for some time it seemed unlikely that we should get back to the *Ville d'Oran* before she sailed, as there was not a boat to be found anywhere. At last some of the sailors of the English schooner yacht *Ione* took pity on us and rowed us to the steamer in the yacht's dingy.

The next morning, February 26th we left Tunis at 10 a.m. It was a glorious morning, and the rocky island of Zembra rose up boldly from the blue waves at the head of the gulf as we steamed out to sea.

A little later, we passed the larger island of Pantellaria, with its white village nestling in thickets of olive-trees and backed by wooden hills. Pantellaria is very little visited, and is said to be a primitive and curious place, but unluckily it has no harbours, and the Malta Channel is a bad place to lie in.

SOON WE REACHED
A ROOFED BAZAAR
WHERE WHITE-ROBED
TUNISIANS SAT.

II

Malta

Arrival at Malta

"Me poor fellow, Sir!"

Bubbly Joe

The people of Malta

The houses

San Antonio Palace

The Governor's Palace,
the former residence of the Grand Masters

Cathedral of St. Paul

The romance of the Hospitallers to be sought
in the days of Jerusalem and Acre

Church of St. John at Valetta, worthy of a voyage to Malta

On the morning of February 27th, I awoke to find the steamer anchoring off Custom House landing in the Great Harbour of Malta. Above us rose the old town of Valetta, grey and weather-beaten, tier above tier of roofs, ramparts, domes and parapets, with the crowning fortifications of St. Elmo overhanging the harbour's mouth; St. Elmo hallowed forever by one of the most heroic scenes in the history of the Knights of St. John. Across the water, within a stone's throw, were the ramparts of St. Angelo (the only fort on the island when Charles V made it over to the Hospitallers in 1530), divided by a narrow creek from the fortress of Penglea; and in the Admiralty creek under the Penglea bastions lay the *Vanadis* in a crowd of yachts and men-of-war. The waters of the harbour were swarming with the brightly-painted *dysoe*-boats with their curious beaked prows and sterns—as picturesque as gondolas, and far gayer; and in among them darted the men-of-war boats, and the launches and gigs from the yachts, making the scene a wonderfully bright and busy one.

We went on board the yacht and were soon surrounded by a crowd of *dysoes* with men selling lace, carpets, statuettes, and all sorts of local atrocities, while one legless beggar propelled himself about on a skiff on which was painted in large letters "Me poor fellow, Sir!"

We soon went ashore in a green-beaked *dysoe*, belonging to a Maltese factotum called "Bubbly Joe," the beak of whose *dysoe* was inscribed with the legend *Bubbly Joe's boat*. This strange individual procures coal and water for the yachts, acts as interpreter and *valet de place*, and ferries the yachtsmen back and forth in his *dysoe*, besides changing money, hiring carriages, and buying everything from lace to Opera tickets.

We landed at the Custom House and mounted the *Nix Mangiare* steps to the Strada Reale, the principal street of Valetta, which runs the whole length of the promontory on which the town is built. The houses are quaint, with their square oriel windows and latticed panes, after the Turkish fashion, but we missed the Eastern dresses, and found the red-coats and the women in their black wing-like faldettas a poor substitute for the gorgeous figures at Tunis.

The houses are all built of the soft, cream-coloured limestone of which the whole island consists, and as their projecting lattices are usually painted light green or pink, the effect is pretty and peculiar. The Strada Reale, however, with its Opera house, its hotels and photograph shops, is provokingly British and modern; one has to wander into the side streets for picturesque effects.

The people are dressed in everyday European clothes, and in fact the reign of the prosaic has settled down upon Malta. As to the Street of the Knights, it filled me with an unreasonable disappointment. I had forgotten that the famous Auberges were probably not built until the end of the 16th or the beginning of the 17th century, and was needlessly aggrieved by their florid, late Renaissance façades, without beauty of detail or dignity of general effect.

In the afternoon we drove out to the San Antonio Palace, formerly the country-seat of the Grand Masters of St. John, lately the residence of the Duke of Edinburgh. The road runs between interminable walls, fencing in the little patches of carefully cultivated green, which reminded us of the story that all the soil in Malta was brought in shiploads from Sicily. This statement, if not true, at least has an air of probability, for there seems to be so little soil in Malta that one wonders how there happens to be any at all, unless it was purposely brought there.

The Palace is rather a pretty villa, enclosed in arcades, and built, I think, in the beginning of the 17th century. It is surrounded by a melancholy orange-grove, in which the trees, being fenced in behind high iron railings, looked like unwilling prisonners longing to escape to a more genial soil.

The next day we went to see the Governor's Palace on the Strada Reale, a large building with long rows of latticed windows giving on St. George's Square. It was, as everyone knows, formerly the residence of the Grand Masters, and in the armoury may be seen many treasures of the Order, such as the original bull of Pope Paschal II founding the Order, the original grant of Malta to the Knights and, saddest and most interesting of all, the silver trumpet which sounded the retreat from Rhodes.

The Council-chamber is hung with tapestry made by Devor-Freres, and bought for the Order in 1713; by connoisseurs I believe it is thought very fine. In the court-yard of the Palace are one or two fine

THE REIGN OF THE PROSAIC HAS SETTLED DOWN UPON MALTA.

araucarias, but the Bougainvillea which climbs upon the walls is a poor, pinched reflection of the wealth of crimson flowers pouring over the houses at Algiers.

On the 29th of February we went out by train to Citta Vecchia, the old town which the Hospitallers fortified before they built Valetta. The railway station is in a subterranean cavern near the Opera-House, and the train, before emerging into the open country, passes through a series of tunnels cut through the walls of the town.

The line runs past the palace of San Antonio, across a glaring desolate country beatified only by frequent glimpses of the sea. We left the train at the foot of the hill on whose top Citta Vecchia is built; and we had a hot climb in the sun before we crossed the moat and entered the streets of the old town.

The old Court House, now a sanatarium for the English troops, stands just within the gateway, on a court-yard planted with orange trees. It is a handsome building, with a fine staircase and galleries, and from the open loggia at the back we had a beautiful view over the island of Malta and the Mediterranean. The steward showed us with great pride the clean dining-room and kitchen, and also the underground dungeons where the Knights bestowed their prisoners of war. The town itself is a miniature Valetta, with the same narrow streets and latticed and balconied houses, enclosed in mighty ramparts. Its desolation forms, however, a strange contrast to the modern gayety of Valetta. Most of the Palaces at Citta Vecchia have been turned into seminaries or convents, and with the exception of a few beggars, the only figures we met were robed in priestly black, and glided noiselessly along in the shadow of the silent houses.

The Cathedral of St. Paul, which was not built until the close of the 17th century, is as tawdry and ugly as only a church of that epoch can be, and contains, as far as I know, no traces of the earlier cathedral built by the Norman masters of Malta in the 12th century. The fact is that, although the Hospitallers are so intimately associated with Malta, that their very name has been replaced by that of the island, they did not come there until the day of decadence, their own, as well as that of art and architecture. The romance of their history must be sought in the old heroic days of Jerusalem and Acre, while at Rhodes the order reached its highest pitch of dignity and honour. When the silver trumpet sounded the retreat of Christianity and civilization from the coasts of Asia Minor, the true power of the order began to wane. There were heroes in plenty, who fought and died for Malta, as others had done for Rhodes, but the Knights, in the flush of their prosperity, had already begun to lose sight of the object for which they were fighting, and were gradually changing from the protectors of pilgrims into something little better than the pirates with whom they contended.

But if the church of Citta Vecchia is disappointing, the church of St. John at Valetta, built only a hundred years earlier, is in itself worth the voyage to Malta. The effect of colouring produced by the rich combination of sculptured stone, relieved by touches of blue and gold, with the soft tints of the tapestry draped between the piers, is certainly unsurpassed.

In fact, I think that the only striking defect is the cutting up of the vaulted roof with the ugly oval windows which serve to light the church. The walls are entirely covered with elaborate carvings of the greatest delicacy, in which of course the cross of the Order constantly appears, and in a place where stone is so abundant and so easily used, no form of decoration could be more appropriate. Some of the chapels of the different orders, which line either side of the nave, are a mass of intricate carving and gilding, and in the chapel of France and Auvergne the walls are sculptured with fleurs de lys.

III

Syracuse

Arrival in a rain storm

Fort Euryalus

This fort, the best preserved specimen of ancient military architecture in Europe

Fountain of Arethusa

The temple of Athene

Sunday services in the saloon of the yacht

The Greek Theatre

"The Ear of Dionysius"

The *Latomae di Santa Venere*

Old crypt of St. Marcian,
where St. Paul preached the Catacombs

We left Malta at 11.10 p.m. on the 1st of March, after four days of June-like weather, with brilliant moonlight nights. We had a smooth run to Syracuse, on the Eastern coast of Sicily, but when we arrived there, at 8.30 on the morning of March 2d, it was raining hard, and with an evident determination to continue all day. It was useless to go ashore, and so we stayed on the yacht, reading, writing and studying the Admiralty charts, which were a never failing source of interest at all hours.

The next morning, the 3d of March, we woke to glorious weather, and at 10 o'clock we started in a flat-bottomed boat for the rivers Anapus and Cyane. We were rowed across the wide harbour and the boatmen, jumping overboard, pushed our boat through the breakers over the bar at the mouth of the stream. Then we glided between low banks fringed with Arundo donax, with cattle grazing in the fields on either side, and here and there a farmhouse guarded by a solitary palm or cypress. Presently the stream narrowed, and we passed under the overarching plumes of the feathery papyrus for which the Anapus is famous, and which grows nowhere else in Europe. Now and then, through the bamboo and papyrus, we caught distant glimpses of the low slope of Epipolae, and Etna's white peak; but for the most part our view was restricted to the low-lying fields about us. It was very warm and still creeping up the river, through a continuous fringe of yellow iris, but when we reached the "azure spring" where the Cyane bubbles up we were disappointed in its clearness, as the rain of the night before had stirred it up and the bottom could not be seen.

After lying for a moment or two in the round basin hedged by tall papyrus, we turned about and rowed back to the yacht. Soon after luncheon we went ashore, and drove out to Fort Euryalus, on the upper part of Epipolae. A bridge leads across the moat dividing Ortygia from the mainland, and beyond this we passed almost at once into the open country.

The road leads through a soft, smiling landscape, full of fruit trees bursting into bloom, olive-orchards carpeted with sheets of lilac anemones, fields of asphodel, and orange-gardens hedged with prickly pear. As we drove along we met a great many peasants in little carts gaily

HERE AND THERE A FARMHOUSE GUARDED BY A SOLITARY PALM OR CYPRESS.

painted with pictures of knights and ladies, saints and angels, and drawn by horses and mules in fantastic harnesses with plumes and scarlet tassels. The road mounted the slope of Epipolae, and from the ruins on the top we had a beautiful view of Syracuse, now confined within the walls of Ortygia, and of the harbour, the Plemmyrian marsh and the fields and orchards which had once been Neapolis, Tyche and Achradina; while to the northward, beyond the hills, we could just discern Etna and the faint coast-line of Calabria.

Euryalus might be called the Greek Carcassone, for I believe it is considered the best preserved specimen of ancient military architecture in Europe. Luckily it has escaped the distinction of being restored, and its walls are now a mass of ruin, feathered with tufts of asphodel, and sprinkled with anemones and delicate scarlet and yellow vetches. The subterranean passages, however, the flights of stairs, archways and galleries, are almost intact, and the places are even visible where the mounted soldiers tied their horses to the walls. We drove back to Syracuse, passing a farmhouse with an orange orchard and a garden full of pink roses and thickets or red geranium, which was my first glimpse of the marvellous vegetation of Sicily. On the way to the harbour, we stopped at the fountain of Arethusa, a melancholy spring enclosed in high walls, and planted with some sickly papyrus.

Then we left the carriage and went for a walk through the town. The streets are narrow and winding, and many of the houses have handsome wrought-iron balconies and carved escutcheons. On the piazza we found the Cathedral, "Our Lady of the Pillar," whose ugly Renaissance façade is placed like a mask before the cella and peristyle of the Doric temple of Athene. It is interesting to see how much of the temple is preserved—the columns of the peristyle embedded in the outer wall of the church, and the cella cut through to form the piers of the nave—and sad to note how brutally the Christian adapter handled his materials. This temple of Athene was celebrated for its possessions and especially for its doors adorned with carvings in ivory and gold; and one of the crimes of which Cicero accused Veres, was the robbery of these treasures which he carried off to Rome.

The Archi-Episcopal Palace, at the back of the Cathedral, has a picturesque inner court, lined with ancient columns, and full of flowers.

The next day being Sunday, we had a short service in the saloon at which the Captain and all the crew were present. The saloon was dressed with papyrus, yellow iris and other wild flowers, and prayers were read at a table covered with the American flag.

After luncheon we went ashore and down to the Greek theatre. It stands on a slope below Epipolae, looking over Ortygia, the bay, and the intervening stretch of olive and orange orchards; a far lovelier view than met the eyes of the Greek audiences who had the crowded house-roofs of Neapolis as a background to their stage.

The tiers of seats, hewn in the rock, are still distinctly seen; but far more interesting to me was the carpet of wild flowers which overspread the whole hill-side; clumps of waxy asphodel, wild reseda, purple and yellow and scarlet vetches, sweet alyssum, wild geranium, snapdragon, anemones, and a hundred others. From the theatre we drove to the "Ear of Dionysius," the sounding cavern hewn out of the quarry in which the prisoners of the tyrant were forced to work. The high walls of the quarry, into whose depths we descended by a steep path, were edged against the sky-line with a jagged mass of prickly pear, and at the bottom grow orange and lemon trees, olive and cypresses, in the wild luxuriance peculiar to the rich and sheltered soil of the Latomie. The cavern, whose ear-like entrance is overhung with dark torrents of ivy, gave forth sundry mysterious answers to our guide's cries, and certainly must have been a bad place to exchange confidence in when the tyrant was hidden in his little chamber at the upper end.

Near the "Ear of Dionysius" are two of the other wonders of Syracuse; the picturesque ruins of the Roman amphitheatre, and the remains of the "Ara," the immense altar 640 feet long, built by that Hieron who reconstructed Sicily after the withdrawal of the army of Pyrrhus.

After seeing these, we drove to another quarry, the *Latomia di Santa Venere*, now converted into a private garden. Here Nature seemed to outdo herself. Sheets of ivy poured over the high stone cliffs far above our heads,

. . . MUCH OF THE TEMPLE IS PRESERVED . . . AND SAD TO NOTE HOW BRUTALLY THE CHRISTIAN ADAPTER HANDLED HIS MATERIALS.

and in every crevice hung clumps of scarlet geranium, cactus, aloes, and prickly pear; while the damper recesses of the rock were clothed in masses of Adiantum. In the depths below, narrow paths wound under orange and lemon trees loaded with fruit and blossoms, in whose shade violets, stocks, hyacinths, periwinkles and pansies grew in delicious confusion. Every turn revealed new beauties. Here we walked between trellises of red and pink roses, there under the shade of a great India-rubber tree, or a clump of bananas or bamboos; the air was stiflingly sweet and every step seemed to crush a flower. High bushes of Abutilon, heliotrope and anthemisia were crowded in between the orange trees wherever there was space for them to grow; while one or two cypresses shot up their black shafts through the sea of bright foliage over our heads.

Finally we drove off, loaded with oranges and flowers, but only to stop at another quarry, this time the garden of the *Villa Landolina*, which seemed still more wildly overgrown with a tropical wealth of flowers and fruit.

We followed a path on the upper edge of the quarry (which was wider and less deep than the others), walking between hedges of lavender and rose-coloured geraniums, while red roses climbed among the cypresses overhead and festoons of ivy draped every rock with green. From this cornice-like path we looked down on an expanse of olives, acacias, oranges and bananas, while at our feet the ground was carpeted with wall-flowers, stocks and heliotrope.

Our next stopping place was the church of San Giovanni, and the very old crypt of St. Marcian beneath it, through which we were conducted by two picturesque young Franciscans. They showed us the fading frescoes on the walls, and the place where St. Paul preached when he "tarried three days" in Syracuse, and then they asked us if we wished to see the neighbouring catacombs.

I have always considered it one of the severest ordeals of a sight-seer's life to have to go through catacombs; and I dare say that some people secretly agree with me. I felt, however, that having dragged my companions through the length and breadth of every garden in Syracuse, I had no right to stand in the way of their apparently genuine taste for catacombs; so in we went. I may as well confess that I walked from one damp tunnel to another as one who had eyes yet saw not; but I boldly assert, on the authority of a guide-book which I read afterwards, that the catacombs of Syracuse are far finer than those of Rome or Naples. At last we emerged again into the delicious outer world *wo alles grünte and blühte*; but the sun was setting and we had lost a valuable hour. We drove on a little farther and stopped at a dismantled Capucin Monastery near the sea. Close by, just beneath its walls in fact, is another quarry, from whose dim profundity tall cypresses stretch up towards the light; a quarry more tragically famous than any other in Syracuse, for it was here that the last remnant of the Athenian army was "destroyed with an utter destruction." It was too late to have the gate unlocked, and go down into the depths, so we stood leaning over the wall for a few minutes, watching the sun set behind the deserted monastery, and then went back to the yacht.

IV

Messina and Taormina

Departure for the Ionian Islands
First view of Messina disappointing
The climb to Taormina
A magnificent view of the Sicilian coast
The mountain village of Mola
Return to the yacht

We found the Spring so far advanced in Sicily, that before leaving Syracuse we decided to change our original plan, which had been to cross over at once to the Ionian Islands, taking Sicily on our return. Instead of this, we determined to see Sicily at once, and leave the Greek islands until later, and we had every reason to congratulate ourselves on this decision afterwards, although of course it took us somewhat out of our way.

We left Syracuse about 3 a.m. on Monday, March 5th and ran for Giardini, the port of Taormina, where we expected to land at about 9 a.m., sending the yacht on to Messina. When I awoke, however, I found that we had already passed Giardini, the skipper having decided that it was blowing too hard to lie to there while we landed; and when I went up into the deck-house at about 10 o'clock we were rushing along close under the Sicilian coast, with the snow-covered mountains of Calabria looming ahead. The sea was a deep blue, smitten with sudden squalls which spangled it over with quickly racing whitecaps, and at every turn of the screw the scenery grew more beautiful as we hurried on through the narrowing straits, past Reggio, and into the harbour of Messina.

We found the first view of Messina somewhat disappointing. The hills about it are bare and inhospitable looking, and the town itself is a conventional modern Italian city, with a handsome line of arcades along the quay. We wished to lie there as short a time as possible, as the harbour has not the best of reputations, so we lunched hurriedly while the yacht was coming to anchor, and managed to get ashore in time to catch the 1.25 train to Taormina.

For two hours or more we ran on along the shore, between endless groves of orange and lemon trees, hedged in along the line by prickly pears, pink geranium and palma christi, with villages half-buried in luxuriant depths of green. On one side sparkled the blue sea, on the other the mountains rose abruptly overhead, while here and there shady lanes led away through the orchards, and flocks of goats wandered down them, driven by the very goatherds of Theocritus, in the "ruddy hide Torn from a he-goat, shaggy, tangle-haired."

We had one or two showers on the way, which flecked the landscape with varying shadows, but the sun came out as we approached Giardini, a little fishing village stretched along a curved beach.

When we left the station, we saw towering close above us the cliff on whose top Taormina is perched, but we looked in vain for the carriage which had been ordered to meet us, and soon concluded that the only way of reaching Taormina that afternoon, was to climb to it on foot. An almost perpendicular and very stony path leads up the side of the cliff, between prickly pears and patches of lemon and olive trees, clinging to little shelves of soil; and it was a toilsome climb of half an hour or more before we reached the long street of Taormina, which runs parallel with the edge of the cliff.

We went to the Hotel Bellevue just outside of the old gate of the town. It is very picturesque, with a pillared gateway, and a palm in the midst of its little garden; but a more intimate acquaintance proved it to be the dampest and dirtiest locanda that I ever set foot in. However, it was lovely at sunset in the garden, which overhangs the sheer edge of the cliff so that one looks straight down at the sea far below; in fact there is nothing in Taormina that is not lovely. The next morning the weather was perfect, clear, blue, and windless, with the warmth of June in the sunshine. We walked through the long street, where women sat in the doorways, distaff in hand, or walked to and fro balancing on their heads the earthen jars which are shaped so much like classic amphorae. The doors themselves are in many cases richly sculptured, and some of the houses have handsome wrought-iron balconies.

At the end of the street a short scramble through a muddy lane led us to the Greek theatre, on a height somewhat above the town. I call it Greek, because it is always so described; but in reality nothing remains of the original Greek theatre but the faintly discernible lines of seats in the hillside; the brick scena and the Corinthian columns are of course Roman.

We climbed to the upper gallery of the theatre, and from there looked out upon one of those scenes which reward one in an instant for thousands of miles of travel.

IT WAS LOVELY AT SUNSET IN THE GARDEN.

To the north, the indented line of the Sicilian coast, with its fantastic succession of peaks and promontories, leads the eye on over the straits to the snowy mountain range of Calabria; southward, through the arches and columns of the theatre, the green valley plunges to the sea, overhung by the time-stained roofs of Taormina; and, over all, crowning the landscape with a wonder and a glory of its own, the white peak of Etna rises into the sky. But no words of mine can give any idea of the beauty of it all, from the cloud of smoke drifting above Etna, to the orchard of budding trees in the depths below; from the columns with their clustering sculpture of acanthus leaves relieved against the blue sky, to the clumps of real acanthus growing at their base; from the rosy hue of the brick arches tufted with snap-dragon and Adiantum, to the golden gleam of oranges over the walled gardens of the town.

We lingered an hour at the theatre and then walked back through the town to the Cathedral square, with its quaintly sculptured fountain where women were filling their classic jars from the nostrils of stone seahorses. On our way we noticed several traceried windows, and handsome Gothic doors.

Another turn led us to an old monastery, with grassy cloisters surrounded by a graceful Ionic colonnade. The custodian showed us the church attached, and pointed out with great pride the fine late Renaissance carvings of the choir-stalls and sacristy, which are certainly worth seeing. The church itself is an ugly, white-washed building, and contains nothing of interest except a curious picture of St. Dominic, sheathed in silver like a Greek *eikon*, and with the order of the Golden Fleece hanging about the saint's neck. After luncheon we started for the mountain village of Mola. I had a nice little donkey and my companions walked.

Our climb began just outside the town, for the cliff of Mola rises as abruptly above Taormina as the latter does above Giardini. The path was very steep, and covered with rolling stones, but my donkey was surefooted, and every turn opened up beautiful views over valley, hill and sea, with glimpses nearer at hand of fragrant orange gardens, and scattered palms and cypresses.

After an hour's climb, I had to get off my donkey, in order to mount the stone steps which form the only approach to Mola. A more inaccessible place I never saw, and every angle of the sheer rock on which it is built bristled with prickly pear, as if to arm it more formidably still.

Inside the walls we found a poor little village, overhung by a ruined castle on the highest ledge of rock. From here there is a wide and splendid view, looking both north and south, but it lacks the concentrated beauty of Taormina. There is, however, one projecting angle from which one can look straight up the valley to Etna, towering close overhead; and as we stood there an icy breeze, most refreshing after our hot climb, blew down upon us from the snow-fields.

We scrambled down again to Taormina in time for a cup of tea; but when we asked for the carriage which had been ordered to take us to the station, we found that none was forthcoming. We strongly suspected our landlord of treachery in this matter of the carriage, and as we were anxious not to pass another night in the Hotel Bellevue, there was nothing for it but to rush down the cliff to Giardini if we wished to catch the train. Luckily we had sent my maid and the bags back to Messina by an earlier train, but even unencumbered as we were, it was a hard struggle to hurry down over the sharp loose stones, and I thought my ankles would turn before we reached the station. We were just in time to jump into the train, and at 7.30 p.m. we were once more on board the *Vanadis*.

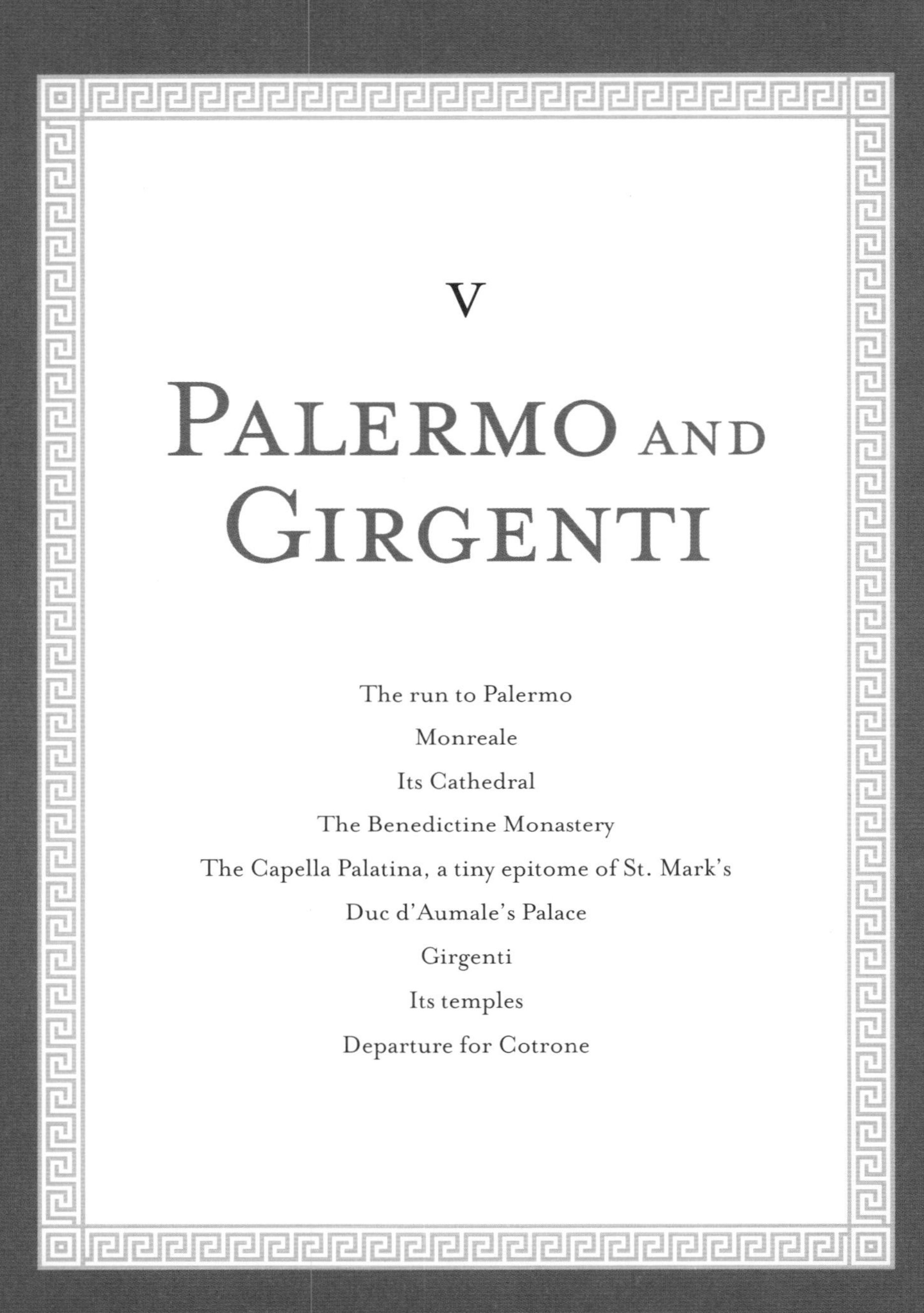

V

Palermo and Girgenti

The run to Palermo

Monreale

Its Cathedral

The Benedictine Monastery

The Capella Palatina, a tiny epitome of St. Mark's

Duc d'Aumale's Palace

Girgenti

Its temples

Departure for Cotrone

We left Messina that evening, and had a smooth run to Palermo, but when I went on deck at 8 o'clock the next morning there were rain-clouds hanging over Palermo, and the sea was darkened by squalls.

Very beautiful, however, were the pale gleams of sunshine on the mountains closing in the bay, and as we entered the port, we had a fine view of the city outstretched between the Conca d'Oro and the sea. We anchored close to the quay, in the large harbour, which seems almost overhung by the great brown mass of Monte Pellegrino, on whose high summit the bones of Santa Rosalia are enshrined.

Unluckily I had such a bad cold that for two days I had to stay on board the yacht, but on the third I was well enough to drive out in the morning to Monreale.

We got a good carriage from the Hotel des Palmes, and started off at 11 o'clock. The streets of Palermo are bright and clean, with prosperous-looking shops, but uninteresting from a picturesque point of view; the only remains of local colour still visible are the gaily painted carts and red harnesses, the shrines with lighted tapers set in the walls of every other house, and the occasional old gateways with carved pilasters and escutcheons, which now seem to lead nowhere in particular.

We drove down the long Strada Vittorio Emmanuele, past the Royal Palace, and through the dusty suburbs outside the Porta Nuova, to the base of the hill of Monreale. A wide road, built and adorned about a hundred years ago with benches, fountains, and the laborious rockwork dear to Italian hearts, leads gently up the hill-side, so lately brigand-haunted, and yet seemingly so prosaic and safe. As we climbed upward we had a beautiful view of the city with its enclosing mountain promontories, while below us lay the rich verdure of the Conca d'Oro. Acre on acre, the endless orchards of orange and fig and nespoli stretched away to the base of the mountains, only broken by the tiled roofs of the farm houses hidden in their depths.

At last we reached Monreale, and stopped at the door of the Cathedral. The Cathedral of Monreale, with Spalato and Athos, had been the chief object of my pilgrimage, and I must confess to a feeling of disappointment when I found myself face to face with it. The exterior I had not expected to like; for that exotic mingling of Saracenic and Northern

THE GREAT CLOISTER WITH ITS ARCADES OF COUPLED COLUMNS
ENCRUSTED WITH JEWEL-LIKE MOSAICS.

invention, which has produced such wonderful interiors, never, as far as I know, created a façade that really satisfied the eye. The curious blending of the two styles is always interesting, and there are beautiful effects of detail in the flat wall arcades of Monreale, but the effect of the whole shows the lack of what the Germans call a *Grundidee*.

The interior is, of course, magnificent, but to eyes accustomed to St. Mark's it lacks depth and variety of colour; it seems to me that for this bright climate it is too much lighted. Of course I know that in saying this I am running counter to the opinion of the highest authorities; but this Journal is written not to record other people's opinions, but to note as exactly as possible the impression which I myself received. The clerestory windows of Monreale are very large and high, and pour down a flood of light upon the beautiful columns and the gorgeous mosaics; but I longed for a little shadow and mystery to break in upon the blaze of colour. From the Cathedral we went to the adjoining Benedictine Monastery and there I could have stayed for hours, in the great cloister, with its arcades of coupled columns encrusted with jewel-like mosaics and surmounted by capitals as intricately carved as a piece of Japanese ivory. In the north of Italy, this cloister would have been planted with Bengal roses and lavender bushes; here it was carpeted with mesembryanthemum, from whose green mat rose clumps of blueish aloes; and no vegetation could have been better adapted to the Moorish effect of the pointed arches and brilliantly coloured columns.

The guard led us next through another cloister to the monastery garden, which overhangs the valley; and what a view the monks had from their marble seats along the parapet! The city on its blue bay lies far below, while close underneath is the narrowing verge of the Conca d'Oro, with the mountains folding in upon its rich orchards spangled with oranges and lemons.

From Monreale we drove straight back to the yacht, and spent the afternoon on board.

The next day, March 10th, we went ashore early and drove to the Royal Palace to see the Capella Palatina. All the hopes raised by Monreale are fulfilled here. It is a tiny epitome of the mystery and splendour of St. Mark's, with the same peculiar dim golden light, and the same bars of sunshine slanting across dusky spaces between sculptured columns; only, instead of the dark alabaster wainscot of St. Mark's, the lower wall-spaces of the chapel are reveted with panels and disks of precious marbles, which carry out the colours of the mosaics above, instead of serving to throw them into relief. In so small a chapel, this treatment is perfect; in a larger building, it produces the effect of cool brilliance which struck me at Monreale. In the Capella Palatina however, the light is subdued by small panes of coloured glass in the windows; an anomaly, I suppose, in Byzantine architecture, but one for which the eye is very grateful in this glaring climate.

From the Chapel we went down to the gardens of the Duc d'Aumale's Palace, a barrack-like building just outside the Porta Nuova. We passed through the *porte cochère*, and as we stepped out on the terrace at the back of the palace a veritable sea of foliage broke in waves of green at our feet. Orange and lemon, palm, bananas, bamboo, cypress and carouba, olive and nespoli, mingled their leaves in an exquisite gradation of tints, overhung by the shimmer of hot sunshine peculiar to the south.

On we rambled between hedges of China roses, laurustinus and cytisus, with the golden and pale yellow fruit hanging in masses over our heads, and the ground everywhere carpeted with blossoming yellow oxalis, coming now upon a stone seat under an olive-tree, now coming upon a fountain smothered in ivy and Adiantum; now climbing a flight of steps to a knoll overshadowed by umbrella spines, whence we looked out at Monreale and the mountains; now entering a tropical jungle of cycas revoluta, yuccas, agaves and epiphyllums; now wandering through shrubberies of oleander, salvia and geranium; but always finding ourselves again under the interminable shade of the orange and lemon groves which seem to stretch out over the whole width of the Conca d'Oro.

We returned to the yacht for luncheon, and started immediately afterwards to take the train to Girgenti. On landing we found the custom-house officer on the quay unwilling or unable to examine our bags, which he said must be passed through the Custom-House; so the servants had to get into the gig again and be rowed there with the bags, while we drove around to meet them.

All this caused a delay of half an hour, and it was only by putting

CAPELLA PALATINA WITH ITS PECULIAR DIM GOLDEN LIGHT AND BARS OF SUNSHINE SLANTING ACROSS DUSKY SPACES BETWEEN SCULPTURED COLUMNS.

our poor cab horses to a gallop that we were able to reach the station in time to jump into the train. The first hour of the journey was delightful, as the line runs along the shore through delicious verdure, with occasional glimpses of Cape Zafferano and the mountains round Palermo. As we neared Termini, a fleet of boats with snowy lateen sails came in across the bay, relieved against the background of blue mountains, and forming one of the prettiest of the pictures which are forever succeeding each other in this most picturesque country. A little way beyond Termini, however, the scene changed, and we turned inland and ran between uplands planted with young wheat and backed by rocks and olive-covered hills. Next the olives ceased, and right and left the wheat-fields stretched away in unbroken monotony, realizing the truth of Hare's saying that Sicily is a very ugly island with some beautiful spots on it. The sun set, and we loitered on from one station to another, thinking how inexpressibly dull Goethe's slow progress across this same country must have been. At last we reached Girgenti at 10 o'clock. We found the hotel omnibus awaiting us, and drove along dark and endless roads, past the lights of the town, out into the country again, and up a steep hill to the hotel door.

The next day we woke to disappointment. The sun was shining, the day was warm and pleasant, but Girgenti, the Girgenti of which we had talked and dreamed, the "splendour-loving Acragas" of Pindar, the "topaz-bastioned city" of Symonds—was this Girgenti? The hotel stands on a hill planted with wheat and vegetables; bleak sandstone hills, treeless and crude, rise behind it; on one side lies Girgenti, an assemblage of dull houses, unbroken by a single graceful or picturesque outline. Seaward, the view is pleasanter; for looking across an expanse of olive and almond trees, cut by a few cypresses, we saw the brown temples rising through the foliage; but beyond these again the dull plain stretches unbroken to the sea. The hotel itself perhaps added to the desolation of the scene, for it bore written on every melancholy feature the fact that it was an unsuccessful speculation. It was opened only a few years ago, and the landlord has been losing money ever since; for who but an enthusiastic archaeologist or architect would perch for more than a day on this mound of artichokes and corn? The dirtiest locanda on a narrow Italian street would have been gay beside such solitude. The peeling stucco of the walls, the dead plants in the conservatory, all spoke of high ambitions and deep failure. Even the Apollinaris had given out.

We had only a few hours to spend at Girgenti, and we therefore determined to devote them wholly to the temples. We drove through the green oasis of almond trees and stopped first at the temple of Concord, the best preserved of the monuments. If arches had not been cut through the walls of the cella, it would still present a complete skeleton of a Doric temple, and yet be no more like the real thing than a skeleton, without flesh and blood, and brightness of hair and eyes, is like a living being. For gone are the sculptures of pediments and metopes, gone is the outer coating of polished marble-dust overlaid with fair colours; and though the majestic outline remains, its glory has departed. In looking at marble ruins one may feel less strongly that they are only ruins, after all; but to me, at least, it was the first thought at Girgenti. How the architect would have shuddered to think that his raw masses of sandstone would remain exposed to the eyes of future critics! How he would have smiled, perhaps, at the sentimentality of those who affect to see in these remains the beauty with which the finished whole was invested! Truly, in admiring the temples of Girgenti: *Gefühl ist alles* ("Feeling is everything").

We drove on to the temple of Hera, which stands on a higher slope overgrown by wild palmetto, with a desolate background of stony hills. Being more ruinous, it is more picturesque than the other. The cella has fallen in, and only one row of columns is standing; and they seemed to me, perhaps because they stand alone, slenderer and more graceful than those of the temple of Concord. Next we went to the vast heap of stones which is by courtesy called the temple of the Olympic Zeus, and which in its day was notable as being built with walls and windows between the columns, as well as for the huge Telamones which supported the roof. One of these monsters still lies discernible among the formless stones. We drove back, stopping a moment in the garden of a dismantled convent on the way, and reached the hotel just in time to collect our servants and bags and hasten to the train. We had a wearisome and uncomfortable journey back to Palermo, and at 10 p.m., to our great joy, we found ourselves once more on board the *Vanadis*.

We had intended to start for Corfu the next morning, but the scirocco was blowing too hard to think of leaving the harbour, and much against our will we lingered on, hoping for a change of weather.

We went to see the Cathedral on the day after our return from Girgenti; that strange and indescribable building with its crenellated parapet, Spanish-looking tower, Gothic ornaments, Moorish mouldings, Byzantine capitals and Berniniesque statues and dome. Inside, it is a waste of whitewash with nothing of interest but the tombs of the Norman Hohenstauffen Kings; chests of porphyry borne on the backs of animals, and placed under canopies with Corinthian columns encrusted with mosaic. We also drove to the neglected Botanical garden, and to the adjoining "Flora," a truly Italian pleasure-ground, with trees stuck in holes in wide alleys, and cinerarias put out in pots by way of flower-beds.

As to the church of St. Giovanni degli Eremiti, whose bells are supposed to have given the signal for the Sicilian vespers, I contented myself with looking at its queer little cupolas from a distance, as I heard that there was nothing to see in the interior, and thought my time better employed in paying a second visit to the Capella Palatina.

At length on the 15th of March we decided that come what might we must leave the unhealthy harbour of Palermo, where we had already lain too long for safety. The scirocco blew with increasing fury, and the skipper and pilot shook their heads over the prospect of going to sea; but it was finally agreed that our fellow-traveller should start out on the yacht, and try to make Cotrone, on the east coast of Calabria, while we took the more roundabout route by rail. The *Vanadis* started out at about 1 p.m., and the wind was then blowing so hard that we expected at any moment to see her put into the harbour again. We wandered about the streets of Palermo, went to the Museum, and spent the night at the Hotel des Palmes, where the wind, howling wildly about our windows, kept us awake half the night. Strange to say, however, the *Vanadis*, on leaving the bay of Palermo, found quiet weather outside and had a fine run to Cotrone, while we were watching to see her driven back to port by the gale. The next morning early we left Palermo and travelled all day, crossing the straits at Messina, and not reaching Cotrone until late at night.

WE WENT TO THE VAST HEAP OF STONES WHICH IS BY COURTESY CALLED THE TEMPLE OF THE OLYMPIC ZEUS.

THE PROJECTING LATTICES ARE USUALLY PAINTED LIGHT GREEN OR PINK, THE EFFECT IS PRETTY AND PECULIAR.

THE ONLY FIGURES WE MET WERE ROBED IN PRIESTLY BLACK.

EURYALUS MIGHT BE . . . CONSIDERED THE BEST PRESERVED SPECIMEN OF ANCIENT MILITARY ARCHITECTURE IN EUROPE.

THE ROAD LEADS THROUGH A SOFT, SMILING LANDSCAPE,
FULL OF FRUIT TREES BURSTING.

THE NEXT MORNING THE WEATHER WAS PERFECT, CLEAR, BLUE AND WINDLESS, WITH THE WARMTH OF JUNE IN THE SUNSHINE.

WE LOOKED OUT UPON ONE OF THOSE SCENES WHICH REWARD ONE IN AN INSTANT FOR THOUSANDS OF MILES TO TRAVEL.

ABOVE US ROSE THE OLD TOWN OF VALETTA, GREY AND WEATHER-BEATEN, TIER ABOVE TIER OF ROOFS, RAMPARTS, DOMES, AND PARAPETS.

ONE LOOKS STRAIGHT DOWN AT THE SEA FAR BELOW.

WE FIRST STOPPED AT THE TEMPLE OF CONCORD, THE BEST PRESERVED OF THE MONUMENTS.

THE TEMPLE OF CONCORD PRESENTS A COMPLETE SKELETON OF A DORIC TEMPLE.

THOUGH THE MAJESTIC OUTLINE REMAINS, ITS GLORY HAS DEPARTED.

SHRINES WITH LIGHTED TAPERS SET IN THE WALLS
OF EVERY OTHER HOUSE.

VI
Corfu and Zante

The sail to Corfu

The American Consul

The Greek Holy Thursday

The procession

Picturesque costumes of the Corfiotes

The King's Summer Palace

"Mon Repos"

The "One-gun battery"

Superb colouring of the cliffs of Ithaca and of Cephalonia

Zante

First sight of the interior of a Greek Church

Relics from the ruins of a submerged city

Sarcophagus of St. Dionysius

Currant vineyards

Zante, more than Corfu, has the stamp of Venice

Celebration of All Saints' Day

Political feeling among the Zantiotes

Chieri Bay

At the Cotrone station we were met by our cook, a polyglot Maltese, who had a carriage waiting for us. We drove along a lovely road, well lighted by gas-lamps, past the walls of the town, and at last reached the boat-landing. Here we had a scramble in the dark over stones and pitfalls of every kind before we were safely seated in the gig. Steam was up when we reached the yacht, and as soon as we set foot on board, we got underweigh for Corfu.

We did not see land the next day until about noon, as the horizon was not clear. By 2 p.m., however, we were among the little islands to the north of Corfu, and each moment as we advanced the scenery grew more beautiful.

Ahead of us, were the Albanian mountains, plunging abruptly down to the sea, their peaks covered with snow, and not a tree or house visible on their slopes, on our right the hills of Corfu, clothed from crown to base in forests of olive and cypress, with villages nestling in the trees. As we rounded the north-eastern cape of the island and entered the straits, the line of the Albanian coast grew less wild, and the hills more fancifully broken, with white towns scattered among them here and there; while just ahead of us, in mid-channel, rose a sharp rock with a white light-house on its crest. We soon sighted the citadel of Corfu, on its bold height, although the town was still hidden from us by the intervening island of Vido. We ran close along the shore, under hills clothed in interminable olive-groves, and the landscape, overhung by a grey sky through which the sun faintly struggled, had an unreal, moonlit look, like the scenery of a dream.

At 5 p.m., we anchored in the roadstead off the town of Corfu, and went ashore in the gig to get pratique. We were allowed to land at once, and a guide led us through the market place to the office of the American Consul, Mr. Woodley—who, by the way, is an Englishman. It was a walk of a few steps only, but it was long enough to give us an *émotion*, for over the shops that we passed we saw our first Greek sign-boards.

The next day the scirocco blew with such fury that we plunged and tossed in the open roadstead as if we had been at sea. The tables had to be swung, and life was rendered a burden by the continual effort to keep on one's feet.

However, we went ashore in the morning, and walked across the Esplanade on which the King's Palace stands, on our way to the Citadel.

Corfu, like Sicily the prey of nations from Pelasgic ages to our own, is nevertheless intrinsically Venetian in all its later associations. St. Mark never spread his wings over city or island, without forever after identifying them as his own by the mysterious impress of the might of Venice. At Corfu, the Venetian citadel, on its jutting rock above the town, dominates the whole scene, from every point of view. We climbed to its top, for the sake of the outlook, which in fine weather must be beautiful, but with the Albanian mountains wrapped in cloud, and the wind tugging and tearing at the olives and cypresses on the slope below us, the scene was somewhat desolate, and we were glad to hurry back to the town.

In the afternoon we went ashore again, and found the Esplanade and the arcaded hotels which line one side of it, decorated with arches and bunting in honour of the Greek holy Thursday. There was a kind of mild carnival going on, and the scene was very pretty and amusing.

A little procession of people in masks and dominoes marched up and down, followed by a few carriages, whose occupants were also in carnival guise; but far more interesting was the crowd assembled to watch the antics of this handful of masqueraders. As we walked up and down the Esplanade, we saw Greeks in white cloth jackets handsomely embroidered, fustenellas of white linen, and red leather shoes turning up in a sharp point adorned with large silk rosettes; Albanians in rough frieze coats, with their belts full of pistols and yataghans, Greek priests in flowing black robes, purple sashes, and curious comical black hats. Still more picturesque were the women. The Greek bourgeoisie wore embroidered velvet jackets, and red caps with long golden tassels. The more elaborate Corfiote peasants had on finely plaited skirts of blue cloth and white chemisettes covered with gold and silver necklaces, and held in place by low bodices of velvet embroidered in gold. Their heads were crowned by enormous coils of false hair with red ribbons twisted through them, and over this they wore white muslin veils edged with lace. Still handsomer were the dresses of the Dalmatian women, who wore long coats of blue cloth covered with beautiful gold embroidery, and sometimes clasped by

IN THE AFTERNOON WE WENT ASHORE AGAIN, AND FOUND THE ESPLANADE AND THE ARCADED HOTELS.

THIS IS THE ISLAND CALLED THE SHIP OF ULYSSES.

one or even two pairs of the heart-shaped Dalmatian buckles in embossed silver, and sometimes they had aprons of lilac shot-silk, bordered with gold and a second sleeveless coat of rough blue cloth embroidered in red; while their hair, braided over each cheek, was simply covered with a handkerchief of flowered silk.

The next morning the wind fell and the day was beautiful. We went ashore in the steam-launch, bought some photographs, a side-saddle and several other things, and loitered about the town looking into the bric-a-brac shops and the little stalls where peasant jewelry is sold.

After luncheon we had meant to take a long drive, but we discovered that the Corfiotes keep the Greek Good Friday in feasting and country picnics, and every carriage was engaged. At last, however, we found a cab and started for the famous "One-gun battery." The road leads between blossoming pomegranates, and sweet figs and olives in their bloom; in fact, no better description than Homer's could be given of the countryside about Corfu.

We stopped on the way at the King's Summer Palace, formerly that of the Lord High Commissioner, when Corfu was under the protection of England. It stands in the midst of neglected gardens, which must have been beautiful when they were well cared for; and even now the thick growth of purple vincas under the olive-trees, and the clumps of yucca and palmetto in the long grass, make the shady walks picturesque and pleasant. The Palace, called "Mon Repos," is an unpretending villa with a terrace from which there is a charming view, over boughs of nespoli and laurustinus, across the blue straits to Albania.

From "Mon Repos" we drove on through endless olive-trees, huge as oaks, under whose shade the soft green turf was thick-sown with anemones and daisies, until at last a turn brought us out on a circular terrace above the sea, the so-called "One-gun battery." Below us lay an almost land-locked bay, called Lake Calichiopulo, enclosed in olive-clad hills; at its entrance a little island, with a white chapel peeping through cypresses, lies midway in the channel. This is the island called the "Ship of Ulysses," which all the archeologists and Homeric scholars beg us not to mistake for the said ship, but which has borne the name too long to change it now.

We drove back by a lower road along the lake, and went to take tea with Mrs. Woodley, who showed us her large collection of Dalmatian buckles, Albanian peasant ornaments, embroidered dresses from Cyprus, and silver yataghans and pistols.

On the 20th of March at 4.15 in the morning we left Corfu and ran down outside of Leokadi or Santa Maura, feeling a heavy swell from the late gales. I did not get up until one o'clock, thus missing a sight of the southern cliffs of Santa Maura, from which Sappho is supposed to have thrown herself into the sea. When I came on deck we were in the narrow channel between the islands of Ithaca and Cephalonia, rushing on through the sapphire-blue straits "under a roof of blue Ionian weather," with the bleak mountains of Ithaca rising on one side, the softer and more fantastic Cephalonian peaks on the other. Never have I seen such colouring in earth, sea and sky. The cliffs of Ithaca, barren of tree or shrub, were stained with a hundred tints of primrose, russet, golden and green, making their bare surface as brilliant as mosaic; while Cephalonia, as we advanced southward, grew more soft and fertile, with deep defiles between the hills, olive-orchards, and meadows of emerald wheat.

We had our luncheon served in the deckhouse, in order not to miss a moment's enjoyment of the scenery; and for the rest of the afternoon we sat on the bridge with white umbrellas over our heads.

As we left Ithaca behind, the chain of rocky islands along the Greek coast appeared in sight, backed by the snowy range of the Arkanian mountains; while ahead we soon made out the dim outline of the island of Zante. As we drew nearer, its irregular peaks grew distinct against the sky, and by 5 p.m. we were nearing the town of Zante. From the harbour it looks like a miniature Palermo, with its row of white arcaded houses following the curve of the bay, and lying close upon the water. Campaniles of Venetian outline, but painted pink or white, break the line of houses here and there, while to the south rises the green hill of Scopo, with country-houses scattered among the violet-gardens at its base.

We went ashore at once to see the English banker, Mr. Crowe, to whom we had letters, and he took us for a walk up the hill behind the town, which is crowned by a Venetian fortress. We passed several churches, of a type which afterwards became very familiar to me, but which I had never seen before, with the upper part of the façade shaped like an open-work gable in which the bells are hung. One was especially pretty, with its gable-belfry painted blue and white, and a mass of white jasmine and pink apricot-blossoms leaning over the adjoining wall.

As we mounted, the view grew very fine, looking across the roofs of the town to the Arkanian mountains, now pink in the sunset, and the Genoese fortress of Clarenza crowning the low ridge of the Peloponnesus.

On the way back to the town we passed a church with lights shining through its windows, and Mr. Crowe took us in to see it. This was my first sight of the interior of a Greek church, and I was much interested in noticing the details of its arrangement. The nave is shut off from the altar by an *eikonostasis* pierced with two arches, and wholly covered by sheets of embossed silver framing the painted faces of saints. In front of this hangs a row of lighted silver lamps, and in the middle of the church stands the Metropolitan's throne of carved wood, with eagles supporting the canopy. It is a handsome piece of work, and Mr. Crowe told us that it was brought to Zante by the present Metropolitan, who carried it off from a village in the interior of the island where it had been for over two hundred years.

Like all Greek churches, it has neither aisles nor side chapels, and the altar is shut off from view by the *eikonostasis*. At the opposite end of the church, a gallery shut off by an iron grating is reserved for the women, the men being alone allowed to enter the body of the church.

The next morning we went to Mr. Crowe's house and saw some Tanagra figurines, and a cuirass discovered somewhere in the Peloponnesus; Greek work of the 6th century B.C., with bulls and honey-suckle pattern of perfectly Assyrian design. We also saw some amphorae covered with seaweed and sponges which had been brought up by divers from the ruins of a submarine city off the southern point of Cephalonia.

We then went for a walk through the town, and looked through various jewellers' shops under the low arcades of the principal street. Here we saw peasant-ornaments, and curious votive offerings representing legs, ears, mouths, ships, &c., on thin beaten squares of silver. We then went to a silk-weaver's house, and after inspecting the looms and shuttles, bought some pretty coloured handkerchiefs. Afterwards, we went to look at one or two Venetian houses with handsome Renaissance façades, and wrought-iron balconies supported on sculptured corbels.

We returned to the yacht for luncheon, and at 2.30 started in a carriage to see the churches and take a drive. We went first to the church of St. Dionysius, the detached campanile of which is a copy of the campanile of St. Mark's. The *eikonostasis* of this church is covered with embossed silver, divided by Corinthian columns elaborately carved and gilded. Before it hang dozens of silver lamps of all sizes, from several of which are suspended large models of ships like medieval galleons. In a chapel on one side of the altar—almost all Greek churches are tri-apsidal—stands the sarcophagus of St. Dionysius, or "box of Denis" as our guide called it. It is a large chest of embossed silver with a bas-relief representation of the Saint's death, and an angel with outspread wings surmounting the lid; but as this Dionysius, Archbishop of Aegina, lived in the middle of the seventeenth century, his sarcophagus belongs to a somewhat uninteresting epoch, and there is nothing very striking about it, except the fact that it is made of solid silver.

Under the latticed gallery at the back of the church, where the women sit, is a long frieze-like painting representing the annual procession on the feast of St. Dionysius, who is the patron saint of Zante, the figures in which all wear Venetian dresses of the eighteenth century. We next drove to the Church of the Presentation of Christ in the Temple. This has a handsome square bell-tower, with two iron balconies, one above the other, just beneath its cupola-like roof. The *eikonostasis* here is even richer than at St. Dionysius; being a mass of wood intricately carved and gilded. Graceful pillars, twined with vines and surmounted by Corinthian capitals, divide the sacred images; one of which is entirely sheathed in embossed silver, while the others, painted in stiff Byzantine style, merely have silver crowns above the saints' heads. Many silver *eikons* hang on the walls, and these, as well as the saints on the *eikonostasis*, were all devoutly kissed by our guides.

CORFU IS NEVERTHELESS INTRINSICALLY VENETIAN IN ALL ITS LATER ASSOCIATIONS.

On leaving the Church of the Presentation, we drove out of the town and through the sunny plain bounded by hills which lies behind it. The landscape was very soft and pretty, with olive-orchards, and currant vineyard, (the currants of the East are, of course, *raisins de Corinthe*), thickly carpeted with a bright array of wild flowers, yellow and white daisies, scarlet, lilac, and purple anemones, dwarf blue iris, cytisus and asphodel. At this season of the year the island, though no longer "wooded Zacynthus," certainly merits its later name of "Flor di Levante."

Presently we found ourselves climbing the hill of Acrotori, under the shade of venerable olive-trees, to the gate of Mr. Crowe's summer cottage. Mr. and Mrs. Crowe were there to receive us, and we walked past the cottage through a garden ablaze with tulips, stocks, geraniums and primroses, to a terrace overhanging the sea. Far below us lay the town of Zante on its curved bay, and across the water we saw the Peloponnesus faintly looming.

The cottage, a low building covered with climbing roses and geranium, stands on a high promontary and from another part of the garden we looked over a silvery sheet of olive-trees at Cephalonia, lying apparently a stone's throw off across the straits. We rambled about under myrtles in full bloom and oranges loaded with fruit and blossoms, while our kind hosts picked handfuls of flowers for us; among them, the famous green roses of Zante. Then we went indoors for tea, and tasted a delicious sweetmeat, a specialty of Zante, made of sesame-seed, almonds and honey, after which we drove home, enchanted with all that we had seen.

Zante is far more deeply impressed than Corfu with the indelible stamp of Venice. The upper class is wholly composed of Venetian noble families, and even the peasantry speak a dialect so much mixed with Italian that I could sometimes understand what they said. A carriage is always called *carroza*, and I imagine that Italian words are used to describe the luxuries of life, much as Norman ones were once used for the same purpose in England.

On All Souls' Day, called in the Greek church the Saturday of Souls, all the Zantiotes go to the Cemetery, and adorn the graves of their relatives with flowers, at the same time placing on each grave a silver candle-stick with a lighted candle, and an open-work silver vase with burning incense. The Archbishop of Zante and all the priests are present and a long service is held. Many of the Zantiote families are very mean, and we were told of one miser, who, when dying, was told by his relatives that he must see the doctor, but at his own expense. He hesitated a long time, and finally sent to ask how much he would have to pay the doctor. When told that the cost of the visit would be three francs, he answered quietly that he would rather die than pay that; and die he accordingly did.

The Zantiotes are much absorbed in local politics, and political feeling runs so high, that any person who is dying is afraid to receive the Sacrament from a priest of the opposite party, lest poison should be administered. No costumes are to be seen anywhere in the island; which seems curious, as in other respects it is much more primitive than Corfu.

At 3 p.m. on the afternoon of March 22d we got underweigh and steamed around the low promontory beyond Scopo into Chieri Bay, which lies south of the town of Zante. It is a beautiful harbour, enclosed in low hills, with two or three rocky islands lying on its quiet waters. We anchored about a mile and a quarter from the shore, in the lee of Maratonisi, a small island overgrown with cytisus, and were immediately rowed ashore in the gig. We landed on a long beach of white pebbles, and walked through a grove of olives to the famous pitch-wells near the shore. Apart from the scenery, which is charming, the excursion presents no great attraction to unscientific people; but it was certainly curious to see the pitch set on fire and pouring out a column of smoke and flame. We strolled back, picking anemones, daisies and poppies in the young wheat under the olives, and before sunset we were on the yacht again and steaming southward to Cerigo. At about 9.15 we passed the Strophades, the house of the harpies, and when I went on deck, about an hour later, we were still bowling on over a perfectly smooth sea, with a brilliant moon overhead.

VII

Milo and Santorin

The start for Milo

Roman Theatre at Tripiti

Exhibition of the holiday dress of the women

Syra, "La Reine des Cyclades," a very modern utilitarian town

Vain attempt to reach Delos

Arrival at Santorin

The islands in the neighbourhood caused by eruptions

The next morning I awoke early, to find a southeasterly gale blowing and the yacht pitching into a violent head sea. It was useless to struggle against it, so we took refuge in a small harbour called Zimeni, on the east side of the Gulf of Messenia. We lay there all day, surrounded by stony hills, which seemed all the more bleak by contrast with the beautiful fertility of the Ionian Islands. I stayed on board the yacht, but the two men went ashore and walked up to a village on the hill, where they were surrounded by the whole population, and hospitably received by the chief man of the place. Their visit was probably an event, for I fancy that even nowadays few strangers go to the wild district of Maina.

The next day the wind dropped, and at 1.30 p.m. we steamed down the Gulf of Messenia, in order to round Cape Matapan by daylight. We ran along under a range of bleak hills, with scattered Mainote farmhouses rising here and there upon their slopes; each house consisting of a square stone tower, with outbuildings, and a high wall around it. As we neared Matapan two boats with scarlet lateen sails stood out picturesquely against the grey rocks. The sea was quite smooth and the sun, which had been overclouded, shone out brightly as we rounded the dreaded cape and ran into the harbour of Port Kaio, three miles to the northeast of it.

Entering by a narrow channel, we found ourselves in a deep oval basin walled in by high hills, barren and stony, but beautiful in outline. A few fishing-boats lay at anchor near the shore, but there were no houses in sight, except one or two walled towers on the heights, and on the slope opposite us a group of half-ruined buildings shaded by cypresses, and protected by a medieval-looking wall. This we took to be the Monastery of the Virgin of Port Kaio, mentioned by Playfair. We rowed over in the dinghy to the beach at the foot of the cliff on which it is perched, but as there seemed to be no way of climbing to it we went back to the yacht.

Having lost two days, we decided to give up our intention of stopping at Cerigo, and at 8.10 p.m. we got underweigh for Milo. It was a moonlight night, with a strong breeze following us, and the air was so mild that we sat on deck until 11 p.m. The wind gradually dropped, and it was almost calm when we came in sight of Cerigo, "birthplace of deep love," whose mountainous outline looked poetic enough in the moonlight to have inspired any number of legends.

When I awoke the next morning we were just anchoring in the harbour of Milo, having been detained in the night by some trouble with the engine. I had read so much of the beauties of Milo that my first feeling was one of disappointment. The usual range of treeless hills, to which the eye becomes accustomed in Greece, stretched around on every side, embracing a wide sheet of water. Just opposite us lay the village of Kastro, a group of flat-roofed, white houses, close to the shore, with a domed church rising among them, which gives an Eastern effect to the scene. Our fellow-traveller went ashore early and engaged a guide and a donkey, and at 10 p.m. we landed, and while the guide, the donkey-man and one of the sailors were engaged in fitting the large saddle I had bought in Corfu, to a very small donkey, we went to call on the English Consul. He lives in a little house close to the landing, and proved to be no other than Mr. Brest, a Frenchman, and son of the Mr. Brest who, with Dumont d'Urville, obtained the Venus of Milo for the Louvre. Mr. Brest and his wife received us with great friendliness, but they had very little information to give us, either about Milo, or the rest of the Aegean. We soon took our leave, I mounted my donkey and we started off. We went up a lane at the back of the town and were soon out in the fields, between stone walls, winding up the hill behind the town. The glare was frightful. The sun beat down from a cloudless sky, its heat unbroken except now and then by a lonely hawthorn or olive-tree. The whole country is a waste of stones, with small terraced fields between high walls, reminding one of the landscape about Malta, except that the fields were lit up with such a blaze of wild flowers as I have never seen before . . . scarlet poppies, daisies, white, golden and pale yellow, blue campanulas, coronillas, cytisus, blue and purple and red and yellow vetches, asphodel and anemones. These flowers, spangling the yellow-green wheat, and relieved against the white walls of the lane and the blue sky overhead, made the brightness of the light all the more crude and dazzling. When at length we reached the brow of the hill, we looked down with great relief over a slope covered with budding fig-trees, to the blue sea and the rocky island of Ante-Melos.

Another short climb brought us to the village of Trypiti, a pile of flat-roofed houses, where we were soon surrounded by the whole population, from old men to babies. The men wear baggy-trousers, red sashes and braided waistcoats laced up the back; but the women have abandoned all vestiges of local costume, except the white muslin kerchief which they wear tied about their heads.

At Trypiti I got off my donkey, and we walked down a steep path to the ruins of the Roman theatre overlooking the bay. The view is charming and the shade of a neighbouring group of olive-trees was very refreshing after our hot scramble. Seven rows of marble seats are visible, built against the hill-side, and some fragments of a marble cornice, with egg and dart and bead and fillet mouldings lie scattered about in the grass. From here we looked down upon the field in which the Venus of Milo was found.

Our fellow-traveller went off with the guide and the populace to see some catacombs near by, while we rested under the olives; and presently a group of women appeared, leading in their midst one who had put on her holiday dress, evidently to show me. She was very pretty, and the costume was most becoming—a figured woollen skirt, an apron bordered with tan-colored lace, a white muslin kerchief folded over her neck and confined by a waist-coat of flowered brocade shot with silver. Over this, she wore a jacket of green velvet edged with brown fur, her throat was surrounded by three gold necklaces, and over her forehead she wore a fold of white muslin edged with gold, with a cream-coloured muslin kerchief trimmed with lace thrown carelessly over it. She had heard our guide say that I wished to see some of the old costumes on the island, and it was very pretty to see the pleased vanity with which she turned about to show me every detail of her dress, and the conscious side-glances which she shot at her giggling companions.

We then went back to Trypiti, and the guide took us to the house of an old man who was evidently a person of importance in the village. We were led into a clean room with a bare wooden floor, and sofa and chairs covered with spotless white dimity. The walls were painted blue and hung with a Greek sampler and several prints. On the floor stood a pair of mar-

FROM HERE WE LOOKED DOWN UPON THE FIELD IN WHICH THE VENUS OF MILO WAS FOUND.

ble feet, evidently a fragment of a statue. From the middle of the ceiling a stuffed flying-fish was suspended, and several small Greek lamps and vases stood on a shelf above the door.

We were placed on the sofa in a row, while our guide, the donkey-man, the chief magnates of the village and the numerous family of our host sat down on the opposite side of the room, and the rest of the population looked in at the open door. A table was then put before us, with glasses, a decanter of wine, a glass bowl full of mastic paste, and some spoons. As this was my first experience of Eastern hospitality, I did not know what was expected of me, but I took a spoonful of mastic paste out of the bowl and then laid my spoon down on the tray, and I found afterward that I had been inspired to do the right thing. The others followed my example, and then everybody had a glass of wine, which reminded us of the "sweet wine" so popular with the heroes of the *Odyssey*.

In our ignorance of Eastern customs we asked what we were to pay our host, and came very near grievously offending him by this breach of etiquette. However we compromised the matter by buying a little lamp and vase from him, and departed after expressing our gratitude through the guide, who probably interpreted it about as eloquently as the immortal dragoman in *Eothen*.

We had intended to mount to the upper village, on the top of the hill, but we had spent so much time at Trypiti that we found that we must hurry back to the yacht, so after vainly bargaining with a peasant for some gold necklaces I mounted my donkey and started down the hill. But if our arrival had excited interest, our going created a furore. Every window, door, balcony and house-roof was crowded with eager gazers, as I rode triumphantly down the village street.

It was 2.30 when we reached the yacht and we did not go ashore again until 5 p.m. We then walked up to see the church in the village by the shore; a tiny whitewashed building with a triple apse crowned with three sugar-loaf domes, and the usual belfry in the gable. Inside, we found an *eikonostasis* quite richly carved and gilded for so small a place, and with numerous votive offerings in silver hung up about the sacred images. As Kastro seemed to present no other objects of interest, we soon went back to the yacht, and at 6 a.m. the next morning, March 26th, we left Milo.

When I came on deck we were coasting along the eastern shore of Siphnos. We ran into the harbour of Pharos, but as there is nothing to be seen there, we steamed out again and made for the island of Serpho. It was a beautiful day and we sat on deck all the morning, steaming between the islands which rose on every side like half-submerged mountains out of the brilliant blue sea, overarched by a sky of palest turquoise. We coasted along the eastern side of Serpho which, like all the others, is beautiful in coulour and outline, as seen from the deck of the yacht, but absolutely bare of vegetation. Not a tree or a patch of green is to be seen on any of the more western Cyclades, only here and there a white village clinging to the hill-side, with a domed church in its midst.

From Serpho we steamed to Kythnos, which is lower and less picturesque than the others. We ran into the harbour of St. Irene, near which we were informed by Playfair, that we should find the ruined fortress of Palaeokastron, on a cliff overhanging the sea. At St. Irene, however, there is nothing to be seen but a large *Etablissement de Bains* built over the hot springs, I believe by the late King of the Greeks. At all events, it is more suggestive of a prosaic German *Bad* than of what we had expected to find in the Isles of Greece, and we steamed out again, and ran along close to the shore, rounding Cape Kephalo, in a vain search for the Pelasgic fortress. But *The Mediterranean Hand Book* proved as untrustworthy as usual, and after convincing ourselves that there was no fortress to be found, we turned back and ran for Syra.

As we drew near the harbour of Syra the sun set in a blaze of yellow light behind the dark hills of the island, while the moon, hanging high over Delos and Mykonus, sent a shimmering path across the waters in our wake. We were wholly encircled by islands, their mountain-shapes transparent in the rosy light; the high peak of Paros to the south, Delos and Mykonus to the east, and just ahead of us the rocky mass of Tenos with the white marble church of the Evanghelistria standing out against the mountain side. As we lay in harbour that night, with the moon shining down on the white town of Syra, piled up like twin pyramids on two rocks above the port, with lights twinkling in every window, we thought it one of the most beautiful sights we had yet seen; and even the next morning as we rowed ashore, the square houses painted blue, green, white and yellow, and thrown into relief by the background of umber hills against which they are built, looked very picturesque.

On landing, however, we were soon disenchanted. Syra, "La Reine des Cyclades" as Gautier poetically calls it, is a very modern utilitarian Queen, less preoccupied with her own charms than with the coming and going of steamers, the loading and unloading of freight, and the noisy hum of business which proclaims her the mercantile center of the Cyclades. While the other islands, an afternoon's sail away, still doze in medieval calm, Syra, placed by accident in the route of the steamer lines, palpitates with the responsibilities of modern life.

All this is a great source of pride to the modern Greeks, but very uninteresting to the traveller who has hoped in sailing eastward to leave the practical realities of life behind. Syra is a hard, ugly place, like all ambitious centres of traffic. The sun beats down cruelly on its steep streets and white houses, and I should think that the inhabitants would give a king's ransom for the sight of a tree. The harbour is crowded with shipping, and the quay is lively and rather picturesque, as the porters wear the baggy blue trousers, red sash and red cap of the other islands. As for the shops, they are very uninteresting, with the exception of the fruit-market with its brilliant piles of oranges and lemons and mysterious eastern fruits floating in oil.

We wandered about the streets, and after buying some *rahatloukoum* (Turkish delight), for which Syra is celebrated, we gladly went back to the yacht.

On the morning of March 28th at 7 a.m., we left Syra for Delos. We cruised about for some time looking for a harbour, and not finding one, ran on to Mykonus, where the statues discovered at Delos are kept in a Museum. But the Captain had no good chart of the island, and as there was no landing place to be seen, we finally concluded to give up the attempt and make for Santorin.

Our reason for taking this round-about course through the Aegean was that at Syra we had heard of the great festival of the Annunciation which was to take place on the 6th of April at Tenos, and had decided to return to Tenos to see it, and to devote the intervening time to the more eastern islands.

When I came on deck we were steaming southward, between the desolate shores of Delos and Mykonus. The day was beautiful, but a fresh southerly wind sprinkled the sea with whitecaps, and stopped our headway a little. We soon saw the headlands of Paros and Naxos looming ahead, and presently we were running down the wide channel between these two islands.

When we were abreast of the town of Naxos, we decided to run in and have a look at it, and we were soon lying to in front of it. From the bridge of the yacht the town looked like a vision of loveliness with its white houses built up against a soft background of mountains. The surrounding country, though treeless, is green and rolling, and in the roadstead just in front of the town, rises the rock of Palati, with the marble portal of the temple of Dionysius on its summit.

There being no good anchorage, we decided to run on, and steaming past the little islands of Heraclea and Skinussa we coasted along the western shore of Nio, and thence crossed over to the volcanic island of Santorin.

As usual the wind dropped with the sun, and the water, though still disturbed by a heavy swell, looked calm as glass as we drew near Santorin. We were quite unprepared for the beauty of the approach, for *The Mediterranean Hand Book* merely gives a few dry statistics about the volcanic origin of the island, and I know of no book of travel in which it is mentioned. In fact the lack of books about this part of the world, though at times an annoyance, lends an undeniable zest to travelling and makes the approach to each island as thrilling as a discovery.

To the right, as we entered the long crescent-shaped harbour, rose the island of Therasia, with a few patches of green on the slope of its cliffs, while on our port side the northwestern extremity of Santorin projected its volcanic wall into the sea.

On its summit the fortified village of Thera rose like an infernal city of Dis, rearing its gray battlements above the scarlet cliff, whose side seemed to glow with the light of subterranean fires. Beyond this a curving wall of streaked and calcined rock closed in the waters of the bay, and the red cliff stood out in startling contrast to the dark shades of the surrounding rocks. A white viaduct built on arches descended in zig-zags from the village above to a cluster of domed houses on the shore, where a few boats lay at anchor in the shelter of the unearthly mass of red rock. The bay itself into which we were entering is, as we knew, the bottomless crater of an extinct volcano, and our regret was great when we found that the only place where vessels could moor was at the further end of the island. We steamed down to a clump of lava-islands in the southern part of the bay, and here we were tied up to a stone pier in a cove between jagged rocks of lava. One of these small islands, called the old Käymeni (or burnt island) has been in existence since 186 B.C.; the second, Micra Käymeni (the little burnt island) was produced by another eruption A.D. 1573; the third, called the new burnt island, made its appearance in 1707 and 1709, while the large island of Therasia, which now stretches like the break-water across the whole length of the bay of Santorin, was torn from the island of Santorin by the same eruption which brought the bay into existence, 237 B.C.

As we approached our moorings the sulphurous smell became very strong, and the pale yellow water (so unlike the blue of the surrounding sea) boiled and bubbled against the base of the lava rocks. This water is supposed to clean copper-bottomed vessels, and there is a row of stone piers all around the cove in which we lay, for boats to tie up to.

The air was very mild, owing to the heat of the water, and we sat on deck until late at night, watching the moon rise behind the black masses of sharply-cut lava.

THE FIELDS WERE LIT UP WITH SUCH A BLAZE OF WILD FLOWERS
AS I HAVE NEVER SEEN BEFORE.

OUR FELLOW TRAVELLER WENT ASHORE EARLIER AND ENGAGED A GUIDE AND A DONKEY.

VIII

Amorgos and Astypalia

Amorgos, its beauty

School at Khora

Search for the monastery founded by Alexius Comenus

Its manuscripts and other treasures

Purchase of jewelry and embroideries at Khora

Character of the people of Amorgos

A feast with the Governor

Local costumes of Astypalia

The next morning I was up on deck at 7 a.m. to see our departure from Santorin. The red cliff looked less infernal in the early light than at sunset; but the scene was nevertheless a wild and striking one. As soon as we had left the bay I went below again and fell asleep, not waking until we were almost in the lee of the island of Amorgos. We steamed along until we made Port Vathy on the west coast, and soon came to anchor in the beautiful harbour surrounded by hills.

We were enchanted by the brightness and fertility of the scene. A white village lies on the water's edge, with one of the conical windmills so common here standing as a kind of outpost on the beach; while in the background olive and fig-trees and sunny wheatfields slope up the mountain-side.

We went ashore for a donkey, and at 1.30 p.m. started off in search of the monastery mentioned by Playfair.

We mounted slowly through the trees, and began to climb the mountain behind the town, between fields bright with wildflowers, poppies, cytisus, scarlet anemones, yellow vetch, pink wild-geranium, dwarf blue iris and yellow and white daisies, mixed with two unknown flowers, one pink, the other deepest blue, wove a carpet of surpassing brightness over every inch of ground. Even the stony mountain-path was tapestried with their vivid colours.

As we mounted higher, we had a fine view over the green valley enclosed in mountains, the village we had left, and the harbour, where the *Vanadis* lay looking no bigger than a steam-launch. Presently a turn in the road brought us in view of the town of Khora, stretched along a high plateau between the hills, and guarded by a long procession of active windmills, while its flat-roofed houses are dominated by a rock rising about 100 feet in their midst, with a ruined watch-tower on its summit.

We wound through a labyrinth of deserted streets and tunnel-like arches, getting glimpses of women with half-veiled faces spinning or weaving in the dark doorways. We had been joined on starting by the innkeeper of the village on the harbour, and as he spoke a little French we found him a most useful companion. He led us to the principal church, a whitewashed building with the inevitable belfried gable, and the usual carved *eikonostasis* within. Then we went to the village school, which the priest in charge invited us to see. As we stepped into the room, a hundred and twenty five little Greek boys rose with one accord from their seats and made a kind of military salute, which they repeated as each member of our party crossed the threshold. They were a nice, clean-looking set, but I should not think that their education would advance very quickly, as we found the priest gossiping with some friends outside the door, while the boys were apparently left to their own devices. We left some money with the priest to give the boys a treat, and continued on our way through the village.

Soon after we left it we turned the slope of the high ridge on which it is built, and suddenly found ourselves looking down on the sea far below, exquisitely blue and calm, with the islands of Anaphi and Astypalaea rising from it in dim outline.

We had crossed the backbone of the island, and soon we were stumbling down a path which zigzagged across the face of the cliff. As we reached the bottom of this path an impassable wall of rock fully a thousand feet high and almost perpendicular stood before us, projecting into the sea and apparently barring our further progress.

I was just beginning to recall the traditional dangers of travelling in Greece, and to think that the amiable innkeeper and the donkey-man would develop into brigands, when we saw two Greek priests in flowing robes on the edge of the cliff high above us, one of whom proved to be the Hegumenos of the monastery that we were in search of. They scrambled down the rough path to join us, their furred garments floating behind them, and a little foxy-faced white dog with large black eyes capering gaily ahead.

As soon as the priests had overtaken us, they led us around the shoulder of the huge rock at a somewhat dizzy height above the sea. When we had turned the angle we found ourselves at a stone gateway surmounted by a wooden cross, and looking up at the sheer cliff above us we saw far, far overhead a white monastery, built in the mouth of a cavern in the face of a perpendicular wall of rock. The building consists of a cluster of belfried chapels and cells, perched on a buttressed wall seventy or eighty feet high, which blocks the whole mouth of the cave.

As we stood at the gate, looking first down at the blue sea far below us, then up at the apparently inaccessible monastery clinging like a swallow's nest to the towering cliff above, we felt that it was worth coming thousands of miles to see. After a moment's pause, the priests led us through the gateway and up the steep stone stairs which climb the face of the cliff. Halfway up we met a man leading a mule with a saddle covered by a white cloth, who had been sent down from the monastery to carry any or all of us up; but we declined with thanks. At length we reached the base of the monastery wall, and here several caloyers (as the lay brothers are called) stood waiting to receive us. The Hegumenos led us up a long flight of steps against the side of the wall, at the top of which is a small arched door, not over four feet high, through which we crept into the monastery. As we entered, I noticed that it was provided with an enormous wooden bolt worthy of the middle ages.

We followed the Hegumenos up a long whitewashed staircase with a tunnel-roof and small cells opening off from the different landings. At last we reached the top, and were led into a whitewashed parlour, where we sat down with the two priests opposite us. Like all the Greek monks, they were ignorant of every language but their own, and the conversation languished in spite of the little innkeeper's gallant attempts at interpretation. In a few minutes, however, the man who led the mule to meet us came in carrying a tray with glasses of water, and liqueur-glasses of mastic, which tasted like paregoric. The Hegumenos then produced a silver tobacco-box and rolled cigarettes for us, and while we were smoking them the servant reappeared with cups of Turkish coffee.

This ceremony over, we asked permission to see the chapel, and after going up and down more flights of stairs and passing through vaulted stone corridors where groups of caloyers stood watching us, we reached the top of the building. Here we found the chapel—a small room with the usual *eikonostasis*, in this case evidently a very ancient piece of work. The faces of the images are quite black from candle-smoke and incense, and the embossed silver in which they are sheathed is of very archaic design. Gold and silver necklaces and other votive offerings are attached to many of them. One *eikon*, which the Hegumenos pointed out with great pride, is

THE MONASTERY CLINGING LIKE A SWALLOW'S NEST TO THE TOWERING CLIFF ABOVE.

WE WERE TAKEN UP A LONG FLIGHT OF STEPS TO SEE A NEWLY WHITEWASHED GREEK CHAPEL.

said to be a thousand years old, and allowing for a slight stretch to make the round number there is nothing incredible in this, as the monastery was founded by Alexius Commenus.

Adjoining the chapel is a terrace, from whence we looked down over the whitewashed parapet at the sea far below studded with the mountainous islands of Astypalia, Anaphi, and Calymnos, the home of the sponge-divers. Passing through the chapel again, we were taken back to the Abbot's room, to see some books bound in gold and silver and some of the richest vestments I have ever seen—a stiff mass of gold and silver embroidery, with haloes of pearls around the heads of the saints and angels. From all kinds of dark recesses the eager monks dragged forth their treasures—gorgeous stoles and altar-cloths, illuminated manuscripts on velum, and other wonders that would have rejoiced the hearts of Curzon and Tozer.

Unluckily we had to hurry away, as our time was growing short. We peeped into the refectory, a kind of dark corridor with silver lamps hanging from the ceiling, and at the kitchen, which is nothing but a hollow in the rock under the arches of the refectory floor; then we said good-bye to the friendly monks, with as much interchange of politeness as the innkeeper's French was capable of.

It would have been interesting to linger another hour, but the town of Khora remained to be seen, and the sun was getting low. We scrambled down the cliff-side, and passing through the stone gateway, took our last look at the monastery far overhead; then we toiled up the further cliff, and approached the town by another path. In the square in front of the church we found all the inhabitants assembled, and a table and chairs were brought out and placed under a plane-tree for us. We ordered some wine, and announced as usual that we wished to buy jewelry, embroideries and pottery. I never shall forget the picturesqueness of the scene; the women with their heads wound in white muslin, crowding in the doorways of the church, the parish priest in his black robe and purple sash, the old hags in dome-like black turbans with white or yellow scarves tied about them; and the throng of inquisitive children pressing about us so closely that we could hardly move or breathe! Some rough bits of faïence and some handsome embroideries were soon produced, which we bought for a few francs; and the competition finally became so heated that one old woman rushed up to us with an empty gin-bottle in her hand! It was impossible to repress a laugh, in which the crowd instantly joined, but to atone for it we made her a little present which sent her away satisfied.

We were next taken to the house of an elderly gentleman who had once been a Greek teacher in a school at Constantinople; a fact which of course made him the representative man of Amorgos. The room into which we were shown was, as usual, immaculately clean, and a silver lamp hung from the raftered ceiling, while a spotless bed stood in one corner. We were asked to sit down, and our host's daughter, a pretty girl, soon appeared with a tray filled with glasses of cognac, and bowls of mastic and orange-peel preserves. By this time, we had grown used to these continuous repasts, and after a little talk, we said goodbye and started for the yacht. The interest we inspired continued unabated, and as I rode down the village street, I was waylaid at every step by groups of peasants with coarse pieces of faïence and beautiful embroideries. We hurried down the hill in the face of a magnificent sunset, and by the time we reached the yacht it was quite dark, and lights were sparkling in the village on the shore.

The next morning at 10.10 a.m. we got under way for Astypalia. We steamed along under the towering cliffs of Amorgos, catching sight of our monastery as we rounded the southern point of the island; then we ran straight across to Astypalia.

This island is not so mountainous or picturesque as Amorgos, but the bay of Maltezana, in which we anchored, is surrounded by a pretty range of hills, and overhung by a bold cliff crowned with a Venetian fortress, with white houses clustering at its base. We were set ashore at once and conducted by a desperate-looking Turkish ruffian in baggy trousers, we climbed the hill to the town, following a path which ran under a row of twelve white windmills, ranged like sentinels against the sky.

We had noticed, on entering the bay, that our arrival excited great interest, for we saw the parish priest, followed by a crowd of peasants, watching our movements from the edge of the cliff just below the fortress; so we were quite prepared for the reception which met us when we reached the town. The governor, surrounded by a dozen Turkish soldiers (for Astypalia is in the Sultan's dominions), came forward to meet us followed by a crowd of cut-throat looking men in Turkish dress, with embroidered waistcoats, and knives and pistols stuck in their sashes.

Soon the inevitable French-speaking inhabitant appeared, and with some difficulty expressed to us the Governor's wish that we should drink coffee with him; and under his charge we marched to the principal café of the town, so closely followed by the entire population that moving was difficult and breathing far from pleasant. We sat down in the wood porch of the café, and the Governor ordered coffee for us and rolled cigarettes, while the attention of the soldiers was divided between watching us and keeping the crowd at bay.

The people of Amorgos have a very bad reputation throughout the Aegean and are accused of making piratical excursions to the neighbouring islands, for the purpose of carrying off sheep and goats; but they are a very mild and civilized-looking set compared with the Astypalians. As we experienced only kindness from all the islanders, it would be unfair to draw any comparisons between them; but I confess that as the crowd of savage-looking faces pressed closely around us in the café of Astypalia, I was uncomfortably reminded of the old days when the Greek islands were not as safe as they are now. We sat in solemn silence drinking our coffee and smoking; then we begged the Governor and our French-speaking friend to order what they pleased, and they accepted our invitation by taking some *rahat loukoum* and glasses of water. After this temperate feast we took leave of the Governor and started to see the fortress; but the crowd had increased tenfold, and our progress was slow and laborious, as the streets were very narrow and dirty, and the populace most unsavoury. Presently we passed under a long whitewashed tunnel into the precincts of the fortress, which, like a miniature house of Jovius, encloses a labyrinth of picturesque streets. First we were taken up a long flight of steps to see a newly whitewashed Greek chapel; then down again, and through another tunnel, until we reached a small square in the heart of the citadel. Here stood a church, with open doors about which a large crowd was gathered; and looking over their shoulders, we saw within, the priest standing before the carved *eikonostasis*, his face pale between the lighted candles, chanting a slow and solemn litany. It was indescribably strange and picturesque—the dim interior, the glow of colour and silver on the rich screen, the blazing tapers and silver lamps, the bearded priest with a green and gold stole on his shoulders, and a black gauze veil over his tall black cap, and the crowd of gaily-dressed women inside the church and around the door. These women were especially striking, as they were the first islanders we had seen in local costumes since we left Corfu. They wore linen petticoats grotesquely embroidered with images of beasts and birds in red and green silks, and some had linen jackets, still more elaborately embroidered, with enormously wide sleeves; while others wore skirts and jackets of scarlet cloth. All of them had *chemisettes* of gold-embroidered gauze, and necklaces of old coins; while their heads were wound in long yellow scarves falling to the shoulders, and forming a most becoming frame to their black hair and eyes.

As soon as we approached their interest in the service flagged, and they soon left the church and gathered around us, grasping the folds of my dress in their excited curiosity. It became almost impossible to move, and we had to beat a retreat to the shelter of the café, while our French-speaking friend apologetically explained that the sight of a steamer was new to the inhabitants of Astypalia. We had previously told our friend that we wished to buy embroideries and faïence, and suddenly as we sat in the café the air was rent with shrieks, and he explained that the town crier was proclaiming our wishes to the public. A crowd of people soon assembled, loaded with embroidery, bowls and vases, old stuffs and gold and pearl earrings. We bought a few things and then, as the sun was setting, we started for the yacht, regretting that we had not another day to spend in Astypalia. Everybody wished us goodbye and bon voyage and the whole populace escorted us to the gates of the town, but here we were left to go down the hill along to the gig.

IX

Rhodes

Arrival at Rhodes

Sketch of the Hospitallers

Damage done by the earthquake and explosion of 1856

Ride to Simbouli

Legend of Dieudonné de Gozon

Some Lindos plates

Climate of Rhodes

Visit to Lindos

Its church

A Rhodian room

The Rhodian peasants, a gentle, friendly race

Safety of travel on the Island

The next morning at 5 o'clock we left Astypalia for Rhodes. The sea was as smooth as glass and the sun intensely hot and as we approached the island of Rhodes we had a magnificent view of the coast of Asia Minor on the one side, fringed by a chain of rocky islands, the low hills of Rhodes on the other and, just ahead of us, the snowy range of the Taurus mountains.

At length we reached the town of Rhodes, which lies on a low point of land at the northeastern extremity of the island, backed by slopes covered with fertile gardens. We passed the outer or galley harbour, and rounding the Fort of St. Nicholas and the Naillac Tower (or rather its crumbling foundations) we came to anchor in the inner harbour, just off St. John's Tower. It is across the inner harbour that the Colossus of Rhodes is supposed to have stood.

All along the water's edge rise the walls, broken by the picturesque twin towers of St. Katharine's Gate, which gives on the inner harbour, and surmounted by minarets, palms, and windmills; while at intervals the circuit of the fortifications is interrupted by battlemented towers, each one of which was formerly guarded by one of the Languages of the Order of St. John.

As the most splendid exploits of the Hospitallers are associated with their rule in Rhodes, I will try to put into a few words an account of the growth of the Order before going on to describe the place itself.

In the eleventh century several merchants of Amalfi founded a hospital at Jerusalem, called the Hospital of St. John, for the benefit of pilgrims to the Holy Sepulchre and out of this modest beginning grew the Order which for centuries defended Christendom against the Ottoman, and whose Masters came in later times to be addressed as "dear cousin" by the greatest sovereigns of Europe.

Many of the pilgrims to the Holy Land, who had received shelter at the Hospital of St. John, remained there to devote their lives to their fellow-pilgrims. They were joined by some of the Crusaders, and in the course of time the hospital provided a strong escort for the pilgrims from their landing until their arrival at Jerusalem. Subsequently, the fleet of the Order escorted the pilgrim ships from the shores of Italy, to protect them against the pirates of the Mediterranean; but this was much later.

In the twelfth century Raymond du Puy, Grand Master of the Hospital, made the Order into a military one, and the chief strongholds of Europe in the East were confided to the Knights Hospitallers.

But Europe failed them in their need, and having in turn been driven by the Turks from Jerusalem and Acre, they were obliged to take refuge in Cyprus in the thirteenth century.

Here they stayed as the guests of the King of Cyprus until their position became intolerable, and the Grand Master Villaret, having cast about him for a suitable home for the Order, decided upon taking Rhodes from the Turks. This was done in the year 1311, and for over two hundred years the Hospitallers lorded it in Rhodes. Their rule was an enlightened one for that age, and the Rhodians were happy under their protection. They fortified Rhodes and Lindos (a town on the other side of the island) and as the Order increased in wealth they converted Rhodes into a splendid and almost impregnable city.

At length, however, in 1522 the Ottoman forces overwhelmed them. They asked in vain for aid from Europe, and after a gallant defense the Grand Master L'Isle Adam sorrowfully decided to withdraw from Rhodes.

For some time the Order was without a home, but at length the Emperor Charles V (who said that "nothing in the world was ever so well lost as Rhodes") deeded to the Knights the islands of Malta and Gozo, which he ruled over as part of the kingdom of Sicily.

Their association with Malta is so well known that it is not worth while to carry this sketch any further, except to add that they might have been there to this day if the Grand Master von Hompesch had not ignobly surrendered the island without a struggle to Napoleon I, who struck by its mighty defenses, remarked as he entered Valetta that it was well for him that there had been someone within the walls to open the gates for him.

As soon as we had anchored we went ashore to get pratique, and as the pratique office is situated on the further side of the galley harbour we had a long row and were obliged to land at some distance from the town. We walked along a dusty road to St. Paul's Gate, and on entering found ourselves close to the old Hospital, now a barrack, just beyond which we entered the street of the Knights, where the Auberges of the different Languages stand.

This part of Rhodes, including the Hospital, the Auberges, the Grand Master's Palace, the Church of St. John and the other public buildings, was formerly enclosed in an inner circle of walls and was called the Castello; while the Palace itself was again shut in by a third line of fortifications of immense strength.

The Street of the Knights is long and narrow, and the fine façades of the houses are broken and defaced by the wooden lattices built out by the Turks. Windows have been blocked, mouldings cut through, string-courses mutilated, and bas-reliefs torn out; in short everything has been done which barbarians could devise to destroy these once beautiful houses. Nevertheless, what remains is far finer and more suggestive of the Knights in their crowning day of strength than the debased late Renaissance Auberges of Malta. Their severe façades, with square-headed openings sometimes surmounted by an ogee arch, were formerly incrusted with marble bas-reliefs (representing the coats of arms of the different Languages and of their Grand Masters) only a few of which are left; but some of the houses are still crowned by a bold parapet.

Rhodes must have been one of the most interesting places in the world before the earthquake and powder explosion combined to destroy the Church of St. John, the Palace and the Naillac Tower in 1856–7. Of the two former, nothing now remains but a mound of stones at the end of the Street of the Knights; and it is fortunate for us that Newton's book was written and his sketches were made just before the year of the double catastrophe.

As it is the few remaining treasures of Rhodes are guarded by the Turks in a manner to baffle the disappointed tourist at every turn, for no one is allowed to walk on the walls, to take a photograph or a sketch anywhere in the town, or even to look at the gravestone of the English Knight, Sir John Newport, in the cemetery outside the gates.

Under these circumstances we found little to do in Rhodes, except to loiter along the Street of the Knights watching the picturesque groups of people, the women sidling by in long striped garments, their faces veiled and embroidered velvet slippers on their feet, the children in bright silk shirts and sashes, the Turks in full trousers with yellow or purple silk shirts, embroidered waistcoats and sashes full of weapons. The colours worn at Rhodes are singularly brilliant and the effect of the passing figures against the grey walls of the noiseless, sunshiny streets, is most striking.

We spent the afternoon in strolling about the town, and discovered in the course of our walk a church—I forget its name—which has been turned into a mosque, and has a doorway framed in white marble delicately sculptured with Renaissance garlands and cherubs, the faces of the latter of course obliterated by the pious Mohammedan; except the escutcheons of the Auberges, it is the only fragment of Christian sculpture that we saw in Rhodes.

The next day, the 1st of April, was Easter Sunday. We had service in the morning in the saloon, and it seemed curious, on our way to Patmos and Smyrna, to read the letter from "the isle that is called Patmos," to the "seven churches which are in Asia."

After luncheon, Mr. Biliotti (brother to the Biliotti who excavated with Newton the Mausoleum at Halicarnassus) came on board the yacht and asked us to go with him to the suburb of Simbulli, a favourite resort of the Rhodians in Spring and Summer afternoons.

A donkey was engaged for me, led by a blue-eyed Greek picturesquely attired in full trousers and jacket of light blue cloth and a many-coloured silken sash; but the saddling of the donkey on the quay drew about us such a crowd of Turks, Jews and infidels, that I retreated to the Street of the Knights and mounted in the august shadow of the Auberges of France and Castille.

Then we started off, passing through the Street of the Knights, and out at the Amboise Gate, surmounted by the escutcheon of the Grand Master of that name. It was on the inner side of this gate that the head of the dragon killed by Dieudonné de Gozon was formerly fixed. It is mentioned in various old books of travel, and Madame Honorine Biliotti, the mother of our friend, saw it as late as 1829. She describes it (in *L'Ile de Rhodes* by Biliotti) as somewhat like the head of a horse, only smaller and

A DONKEY WAS ENGAGED FOR ME.

WE PASSED THROUGH THE STREET OF THE KNIGHTS AND OUT AT THE AMBOISE GATE.

flatter, with something serpent-like in the outline. When she saw it the lower jaw had fallen away. In 1837 this head had disappeared.

The legend of Dieudonné de Gozon is well known; how he disobeyed the Grand Master's orders and set about to devise means of killing the dragon or serpent which infested the island and had already slain the flower of the Knights; how he retired to his father's castle and trained his English bull-dog to attack a counterfeit presentment of the beast; then how he returned to Rhodes and with his dog's help killed the dragon, and brought his head in triumph to lay at the Grand Master's feet. It is also known how he was expelled from the Order for his disobedience, only to be reinstated with double honours, and afterwards made Grand Master; but the curious testimony in favour of the legend is generally overlooked.

In the first place, on the tomb of Dieudonné de Gozon, which was erected only thirteen years after his death, he is described as the Knight who "slew an enormous serpent;" in the second place we have the witness of several people that the head of the animal was to be seen affixed to the Amboise Gate as late as 1829. There are many explanations of the story, but the most probable one is that the dragon was a large crocodile which escaped from some shipwrecked vessel on the coast of Rhodes. At all events it is certainly strange that the Knights of St. John should have believed thirteen years after Gozon's death, which occurred, by the way, as late as the fifteenth century . . . that he really "slew an enormous serpent." Passing out of the Amboise Gate, we went through a long line of Turkish cemeteries with toppling headstones crowned by carved turbans and leaning every which way in a tangle of wild flowers and grass. Beyond this, the way to Simbulli lies through the high-walled lanes of the Greek suburb (for the Christian Rhodians are all compelled to live outside the walls) and thence at last into the open country. And what a lovely country it is! As we mounted higher, we looked down over the sunny gardens stretching below us to the sea, and enclosing the town in a mass of foliage—orange and fig and olive—broken here and there by the brilliant rose-coloured clouds of the blossoming Judas trees. Torrents of ivy poured over the walls, the road was edged with daisies, poppies and cyclamen, and there was a look of luxuriant verdure about the whole landscape which was very refreshing after the white glare of the barren cyclades. No wonder that the heart of L'Isle Adam yearned over Rhodes, and that he hesitated and temporized long before abandoning all hopes of its recovery and accepting instead the desolate rock of Malta.

At length we came to a field of young wheat in a hollow shaded by turpentine trees (*Pistacia terebinthus*) and here Mr. Biliotti made us stop and examine a group of empty Greek tombs in a very ruinous state, half muffled in climbing leafage.

Then we went on by more leafy lanes, and at last reached the little café of Simbulli, built on a terrace shaded by great plane-trees. Nothing can be imagined more deliciously cool and green than this place, nor more picturesque than the little stream close by, shaded by overleaning trees and spanned by the arch of a Roman aqueduct. We sat there for a long time on a stone bench against the wall of the house, drinking Turkish coffee, and listening to the tinkle of water into a square tank under the plane-trees; then we returned to Rhodes by a lower road, and stopped on our way at the English Consulate to see some Lindos plates.

The first of these plates, which were made at Lindos in the time of the Knights, are supposed to have been the work of Persian prisoners, as they are ornamented with Persian designs, and one of the oldest in existence is inscribed with the words "how long shall we linger in exile," in Persian letters. In the later plates, the same style of coloring and ornamentation was invariably followed. Some of them are very valuable, but of course all the best have long since been bought by Museums and private collectors, and only very ordinary ones are to be found in Rhodes.

The next morning Mr. Biliotti and his son came on board the yacht and at 8 o'clock we got underweigh and ran around the island to Lindos. The day was perfect and the Mediterranean smooth as the "glassy sea" of the Apocalypse. In fact our two days in Rhodes convinced us of the truth of the saying that it has the most beautiful climate in the Mediterranean.

In about three hours we reached Lindos, on the east side of the island. Its fine harbour is guarded by a promontory on whose high cliff stands the Citadel of the Knights, in which Villaret shut himself up when he defied the Order; but the town is hidden in a hollow behind this promontory, and only a few houses in gardens are seen as one approaches from the sea.

As soon as we had anchored we were set ashore and climbed up the road to the town under a blazing sun. The houses of Lindos are low and flat-roofed, but most of them date from the time of the Knights, and many handsome doors and windows are to be seen, generally square-headed, with the Byzantine rope or scroll-moulding, but sometimes surmounted by flamboyant tracery in an ogee arch. Unluckily these houses have all been whitewashed, which of course destroys the effect of the carving.

We were first taken to see the church, which is not described in any book of travel that I have read, and is merely mentioned by Newton. He calls it Byzantine, but unless he uses the term geographically, as dividing the East from the West, I don't see what he means. The church consists of a nave with pointed tunnel-vaulting, a semi-circular apse, and a dome over the intersection of the nave and transepts. The *eikonostasis* does not form a structural part of the church, but is merely a screen put up in front of the apse. It is evident that the pointed tunnel-vaulting of this church must have traveled from the East to the West and back again, instead of being taken direct from the Saracen, like the pointed arches of Monreale and Lazisa. Rhodes was taken in 1311, and Fulk de Villaret, who conquered it, was a Knight of Provence. The church of Lindos was probably built in his day or in that of his successor, Helion de Villeneuve, Grand Prior of St. Gilles in Provence; and as late as the middle of the thirteenth century the churches of Provence were all built with pointed tunnel-vault roofs. The church of Lindos, therefore, which was probably built not later than the first quarter of the fourteenth century, under the rule of Provençal Grand Masters, and most likely from the designs of Provençal architects, is apparently a faithful reproduction of the style which everywhere prevailed in the mother country at least until within fifty years of that time. If this is the case, the pointed arch of Lindos has performed a double journey, having been carried to Provence from the East either by the Greeks, or in later times by Provençal travelers, and taken back to

Saracenic lands by the very Provençals who first made it known to western Europe. To call this church Byzantine is absurd. Pointed arches, it is true, were used in the Byzantine basilica of Monreale, but they were an accidental divergence from the Byzantine forms, which are essentially round-arched, and the accident which produced them—the strange blending of Norman and Saracenic forms in Sicily—was one which had no counterpart elsewhere.

The interior of the church is at present wholly covered with archaic looking frescoes in small panels. Grotesque as they are, and freshly covered with a raw daubing of paint, the effect produced is rich and brilliant, as that of painted interior always is.

In front of the *eikonostasis* hangs a very handsome chandelier of brass, surrounded by numerous silver lamps, and the floor is laid, after the Rhodian fashion, with black and white pebbles in elaborate designs.

From the church we mounted to the top of the cliff on which the Citadel stands. The sides of this cliff were covered with sheets of wild flowers, and we left the servants there to gather bouquets for the yacht.

The walls and battlements of the Citadel are still standing, but the interior is a confused mass of stones. One room, however, is still standing, probably the guard-room, or dining-hall, with a chimney-piece painted in fresco with various coats of arms, among which we noticed the Cardinal's hat of the Grand Master d'Aubusson.

There are also some remains of the chapel, a small building with aisles and triple apse; and Mr. Biliotti carefully pointed out to us the chaotic ruins of the Greek temples on which the Christian fortress was built.

After lingering for some time to look out over the splendid view, we scrambled down to the town again, and our guide invited us to go to his house.

Like all the others in Lindos, it was divided from the street by a high white wall, and a courtyard prettily paved with black and white pebbles. In one corner of this court stood a large orange-tree, loaded with fruit and blossoms, and we gladly accepted the invitation we received to help ourselves to some of the delicious oranges, which tasted like nectar after our hot walk. While we were eating them, our guide's wife set out basins, towels and a pitcher of water on the stone bench against the wall of the house, and after we had washed our hands we went indoors.

The room into which we were shown was exquisitely clean, and as it is a typical Rhodian room I will describe it. The floor is paved with black and white pebbles, and across the wall of the room opposite the door runs a long wooden bench. At one end of this is a raised wooden dais, and on this again a higher dais, set in the angle of the walls and forming a bed. This bed should be hung with linen draperies and mosquito-curtains heavily embroidered in red and green silks, but such adornments are rarely seen nowadays. On either side of the door are two lower wooden platforms, also used as beds, and the bedding consists of a heap of rugs and pillows. The ceiling (which in this case, like the house, dates from the time of the Knights) is of carved cedar-wood, elaborately painted and gilded, and presenting a strange contrast to the whitewashed walls. A foot or two under the ceiling a narrow wooden shelf runs all around the walls, with plates ranged upon it, all of which were formerly of Lindos ware. Now they are replaced by cheap modern pottery, except on the side facing the door, where a double row of Lindos plates is generally to be seen. An oil-lamp hangs by a chain from the middle of the ceiling, and a bright Makri rug is spread on the floor.

As usual we were given some delicious coffee, which we drank surrounded by the watchful family of our host. The Rhodian peasants are a gentle, friendly race, and robbery is almost unknown on the island. The women wear no distinctive dress, and their pale, worn-looking faces are uncovered. Travelling all through the island is said to be perfectly safe, but the roads are so bad that even on a mule it is said to be far from comfortable, and carriages are of course unknown.

We went to several more houses like the one I have described, and finally returned to the yacht, and reached the harbour of Rhodes at nightfall.

WE LINGERED SOME TIME
TO LOOK OUT
OVER THE SPLENDID VIEW.

X

Tenos and Patmos

Anchorage at Vathy

Naxos

Temple of Dionysius at Palati

Festival of the Annunciation

The most popular fête in Greece

Anniversary of Greek Independence falls upon the same day

Reception given the travellers

Church of the Evanghelistria

A wonderful procession

Arrival at Patmos

Expense of a view of the body of St. John

Coffee with the Greek Consul

Cave of the Apocalypse

On the morning of April 3d at 7 o'clock we left Rhodes, and steamed back to Astypalia, where we anchored for the night in the harbour of Vathy. We left Vathy at daylight on the 4th, and ran back to Naxos, where we came to anchor at about 2 p.m.. We went ashore and looked about the town a little, but it is dull and uninteresting and the people were a disagreeable-looking set. We then rowed to the rock of Palati, and inspected the marble doorway of the temple of Dionysius, after which we returned to the yacht. Near us lay a picturesque brig, which was to carry a load of passengers to the festival of Tenos, and all the afternoon boatloads of peasants with rugs, mattresses and provisions were being taken on board. We were also visited by a boatful of people, evidently the *haut ton* of Naxos, for the young ladies spoke French and Italian, and wore modern-looking dresses. I asked one of them if she was going to Tenos, where upon she answered with a shudder: "*Nous sommes orthodoxes,*" and it turned out that there is a Catholic convent at Naxos where all the young girls are educated—the convent and the Italian speech being of course both relics of the time when Naxos was an Italian duchy. Elegant as our visitors were, however, they did not disdain to bring with them for sale a bundle of embroideries and old clothes, among which were one or two beautiful Empire dresses of satin embroidered with flowers in coloured silks.

We lay at Naxos all that afternoon and night, getting underweigh for Syra at 5 a.m. on the 5th. There was a fresh southerly wind blowing and when we reached Syra, we found that the rough sea had frightened many people away from Tenos, where there is only an open roadstead fully exposed to the south. At Syra we took on board the American Consul, and a soiled but amiable Greek called Eulambios, who had been obliging enough to send his servant the day before to the Mayor of Tenos, with a letter from the Governor of the Cyclades to announce our arrival. At 4 p.m. we started for Tenos, arriving at about 5.15. The wind had dropped, but a huge sea was rolling in, and we were some time picking up an anchorage among the steamers, schooners and various craft which were bobbing up and down on every side of us. We had to land in a shore-boat, and we bounced about so much that our Greek friends were rather

BRASS AND SILVER EIKONS, PICTURES PAINTED ON WOOD.

unnerved, and we had some difficulty in landing at the jetty, where the Mayor received us with great politeness. Several steamers from the Peiraeus, Asia Minor and Syra were already at anchor or just coming in, and the roadstead was swarming with boats to carry the pilgrims ashore. We were told that these poor people, who can go to Tenos and back in any of the large steamers for a franc, are nearly ruined by the extortionate charges of the boatmen at Tenos, who realize that the pilgrims are completely in their power, as the steamers do not provide any boats.

The Greek festival of the Annunciation at the Church of the Evanghelistria at Tenos is the most popular fête in Greece and as the anniversary of the Greek declaration of Independence falls on the same day, the two events are celebrated together. The name of the Church means "Our Lady of Good Tidings," and it is called so from a miraculous image of the Virgin which, in fulfillment of a nun's dream, was found in the neighbourhood in 1824. About 30,000 pilgrims come to Tenos annually for the two festivals of the Annunciation and Assumption, from the mainland of Greece, Albania, Asia Minor, and all the islands. They are lodged at the expense of the Church, but bring their food and bedding with them, and the Church receives an annual revenue of about 100,000 francs from their offerings.

As soon as we landed we started off through the town, preceded by the Mayor and a soldier to clear the way. The scene on the quay was very picturesque. It was crowded with peasants, many of them carrying their rugs, boxes and mattresses on their backs, others seated in groups at little tables before the cafés. Those from the interior of Greece were the most noticeable—the women in long white linen gowns, embroidered in coloured silks, with sleeveless outer coats of white cloth embroidered in dark blue or green, and necklaces of gold and silver coins about their necks. They wore their hair in two braids plaited with strands of wool which fell in large tassels at the ends, a small orange-coloured cap over the forehead, sometimes edged with a fringe of coins, and over this a flowered silk kerchief. Some had wide gold bracelets set with turquoises, and their coats were clasped with gold and silver buckles. The men wore fustanellas, belts full of weapons, sheep-skin coats, and Greek caps. The women from Asia Minor were conspicuous for their embroidered velvet jackets and petticoats of flowered stuff, and there were several other varieties of costume which I had hardly time to notice. We walked up the long street leading from the quay to the Evanghelistria and lined with booths decorated with oleander boughs, where the peasants were buying brass and silver *eikons*, pictures painted on wood, candles, rosaries, and little tin cans in which to carry away holy water. Through the crowd moved peddlers carrying trays full of silver votive offerings, and deformed beggars exhibiting their horrible distortions. The feast fell on a Friday, on which day meat is forbidden in the Greek church, even if it is a festival; and the market-booths were accordingly piled with olives, figs, oranges, sesame-seed and honey, and fish in oil.

At the upper end of the street we passed under a white archway and found ourselves in the large courtyard of the Evanghelistria. It is surrounded on all sides by a two-storied white building with arcades, containing 110 rooms in which the pilgrims are lodged, and in one angle of the enclosure stands the church, an imposing marble building, also two stories in height, and flanked by arches. A handsome double staircase leads to the upper church, below which are chapels used as lodgings for the sick pilgrims, who are supposed to be cured by the holy air. We put our heads into one of these lower chapels, which was packed with people, and the atmosphere was such that if they are not cured they must certainly be killed. In the cloistered courtyard the scene was very gay. It was full of peasants strolling about under the palms and cypresses, gossiping around the marble fountains, or unpacking their bundles of bright-coloured rugs and bed-quilts. We went up to the church, and the Mayor and the soldier pushed us through a dense mass of people to the spot where the miraculous Virgin was exposed to view. It is a small *eikon* covered with gold and diamonds and enclosed in a glass case which was surmounted by a wreath of orange-blossoms. The church was blazing with lighted tapers, and seemed to be a mass of gold and silver and hanging lamps, but though we struggled through its whole length, I could not take in any of the details of its arrangement. We were next taken to the apartments of the Commissioner of revenues of the church, and here in a large room overlooking the cloisters we went through the usual well-meant but wearisome coffee drinking. Then we went back to the yacht for dinner.

At 9 p.m. we went ashore again, and returned to the church. Its façade and bell-tower and all the arcades were brightly illuminated, and rockets, Roman candles and Catherine wheels were blazing up in every direction. We walked through the courtyard, which was crowded with peasants stretched out under the palm-trees fast asleep, in blissful ignorance of the rockets whizzing over their heads, while under the arcades there was a solid mass of sleeping people spread out on rugs and mattresses, and sometimes so closely huddled together that there was not room enough for them to lie down. We then went up to the terrace adjoining the Commissioner's rooms, and looked out on the brilliantly-lighted church, the courtyard full of people lying under the dark trees, and overhead the starlit sky, through which the fireworks flashed incessantly.

The following morning the fête really began. The men-of-war of the Greek squadron arrived early, and they and the *Vanadis* and all the other ships in the roadstead were dressed with flags. We went ashore early, and this time found the Mayor awaiting our arrival with white gloves on and a gold-headed stick, and accompanied by the Chief of Police in full uniform, and half a dozen soldiers. Thus escorted, we had no difficulty in making our way through the crowd, although it had been greatly increased by the arrival of several other steamers. We walked up the long street, which in anticipation of the coming procession was already lined with a double row of sailors and of Greek chasseurs in snow fustanellas, embroidered jackets and silver buttons, and on reaching the church we found that some seats had been reserved for us near the door. But although the Archbishop was celebrating mass, and the gleaming of lights and vestments was very alluring, the unbearable heat and crowd soon drove us out into the air again, and back we hurried to the Mayor's house on the quay. Here we were led upstairs to a room full of Greek ladies and placed in a window overlooking the quay, where for an hour or more we waited for the procession.

At last it came, and as it approached the dense crowd in the square below us became agitated by one common movement, men,

THE SCENE ON THE QUAY WAS VERY PICTURESQUE.

A GROUP OF PRIESTS IN GORGEOUS ARRAY.

women, and children all crossing themselves with frantic continuity as long as the miraculous Virgin remained in sight. It was a wonderful scene, with the mass of brightly-dressed people, in which the white gowns of the women and the scarlet caps of the men recalled the vivid poppies and daisies of a Greek wheat field, the continual movement of hundreds of devout heads and hands, and the background of blue sea and gaily-adorned ships which closed the picture in. And in the midst of this setting the procession suddenly appeared—first a military band, then men carrying silver lanterns and crosses, and embroidered banners—then the Mayor and Naval officers, and (to our astonishment) the fat pilot who had brought us over from Syra and who evidently occupied a place of honour in the procession. After him followed two priests bearing on high our Lady of Good Tidings, at sight of whom a fresh wave of devotion overswept the crowd, and lastly the Archbishop in vestments of white and gold, a golden mitre on his head, a silver crucifix in one hand and the patritza in the other, surrounded by a group of priests in gorgeous array, and followed by acolytes in robes of green silk.

In the middle of the square the procession paused, and the Archbishop, lifting up the crucifix, intoned the Te Deum, to which the priests responded. Then came some allusion to the Greek Independence, and to the King and Queen, at which the people cheered loudly, and the procession then moved on and disappeared.

We hurried back to the yacht, and after giving luncheon to the Mayor and Commissioner, we got underweigh for Delos. The pilot assured us that he knew the harbour well, but after anchoring in a little bay and going ashore, we found ourselves on the neighbouring island of Rhenia, and the pilot then confessed that he could not undertake to find an anchorage off Delos. So completely has the glory of Delos departed that the average Greek does not know it from Rhenia, and both are called indifferently by the same name.

We reached Syra again at twilight, and all that evening we watched the illumination and fireworks in the town from the deck of the *Vanadis*.

At 5 a.m. on the 7th of April we left Syra for Patmos, arriving at about 3 p.m. The day was perfect, the sea as smooth as a lake and of the deepest sapphire, as Patmos rose before us out of the encircling islands—for our "holy isle" is as closely surrounded as Delos. The island of Patmos is one of the most beautiful in the Egean—a long narrow range of mountains, so deeply indented with bays and fjords as to be almost cut in two by the sea; and the town stands on a hill overlooking one of the loveliest of these natural harbours. Above the houses rise the battlemented walls of the fortified Monastery of St. John the Divine, and half way down the hill is a small church built over the cave where he is supposed to have seen "a door opened in Heaven."

We went ashore at once, and I found a donkey to carry me up the hill to the town. We passed through the small village by the harbour, and crossed a narrow strip of land with the sea on each side, from the further end of which a steep road, made of slippery blocks of granite, leads up to the town. The views all the way up are beautiful, but the town itself is dull and deserted-looking.

We mounted to the highest point, and climbing a flight of stone steps passed under a vaulted archway and found ourselves in the cloister of the monastery. This cloister is enclosed in a round-arched arcade, and some of the arches are supported on Moorish-looking spirally-fluted marble columns, while several flying pointed arches are thrown across the width of the cloister, probably as a precaution against earthquakes. We were next taken up and down numerous flights of stairs, until we reached the parlour of the Hegumenos, where coffee, sweetmeats and cigarettes were consumed in solemn silence. The room was bare and ugly, but there were one or two Byzantine frescoes on the walls, and many more were doubtless hidden under the all-pervading whitewash. Having finished our coffee, we mounted to the top of the walls, and looked down over the high battlements at the whole island outspread beneath us on the peaceful sea.

The monastery is a very fine specimen of a fortified monkish stronghold of the middle ages, and everything is in a perfect state of preservation. In passing through one of the arcaded galleries I noticed the bar of wood and the bent piece of iron and wooden hammers which the Turks at one time compelled the Greek monks to use in the place of bells.

From the battlements we were again led down to the cloister and taken into the church which forms one side of it. The outer walls of the church are covered with grotesque Byzantine frescoes, and three small doorways with beautifully carved doors of wood lead into the narthex, a dark and narrow room, in which we could barely perceive a dim gleam of lamps and *eikons* and golden haloes. The church itself is very small and dim, with round arches supported on piers, and an *eikonostasis* of remarkable richness. The church furniture is all of wood inlaid with mother-of-pearl, and many handsome silver lamps hang from the ceiling. The Hegumenos was anxious to show us the body of St. John, which is said to be enclosed in a painted tabernacle in the narthex, but as our guide told us that the privilege would cost us £4, we found some excuse for declining it.

Having wished the friendly monks goodbye, we left the monastery, and strolled through the town in a vain search of curiosities, and presently we were overtaken by an old man who told us in English that the Greek Consul begged we would go to his house to drink coffee. "More coffee!" was our first ungrateful thought, but there was no help for it, so we followed our new acquaintance to the Consul's house, and passing through a flower-filled loggia entered the room where that gentleman and his family were waiting to receive us. They were simple people who welcomed us most kindly, and as the Consul spoke Italian, we got on very well together. The room was large and bare, but the sofas on which we sat were covered with beautiful embroidered bed-hangings and there were some handsome bits of silver on the table. A young girl presently appeared carrying a silver tray with a bowl of brandied cherries, graceful Venetian glasses full of orange-flower water and a little silver plate with spoons on it, and luckily for us these messes were followed by some excellent coffee.

Soon afterwards we took our leave and departed as usual loaded with bouquets which the silent but interested women of the family had picked for us in the loggia.

The next morning was Sunday, and we were disappointed to find a dark, cloudy sky overhead, for after twenty days of continuous sunshine we had grown to expect fine weather as a matter of course; but after all no rain fell.

We sent part of the crew ashore in the morning to see the cave of the Apocalypse, and the rest in the afternoon; and at 2.30 p.m. we ourselves climbed up the hill to see it. A small white building on a rock covers the site of the cave, and going in under the usual archway to a picturesque court full of geraniums and rose-bushes, we were welcomed by the priest and his family. They led us down a long flight of winding steps, which seemed to descend into the depths of the earth, and at the bottom of which we found ourselves in a small chapel, built into the cavern itself, and partly roofed by an overhanging mass of rock. It is dark, and full of votive offerings, and the place was pointed out to us where St. John's head had rested, as well as a cross which he had carved in the rock; in addition to which, a toothless old lady of the priest's family, gave me a bit of the stone wrapped up in a paper.

On mounting again to the court, we were, of course, taken into the priest's parlour, which looks out over a pretty terrace, but this time we got off very easily with some quince marmalade and a glass of water. Then we returned to the yacht, laden as usual with orange-blossoms, stocks and geraniums. Late that afternoon as we were sitting in the deck-house, a dirty-looking man rowed up to the *Vanadis*, and coming on board produced a still dirtier parcel wrapped in newspaper which he told us was from the *Papa*; and it turned out to be, in fact, a bottle of orange-flower water from the kind old priest of the Apocalypse. After wondering for a long time what to send in return, we filled a tin box with candied fruit and entrusted it to the *Papa*'s messenger; and judging from the amount of sweetmeats eaten in the East, I doubt if we could have found a more welcome present.

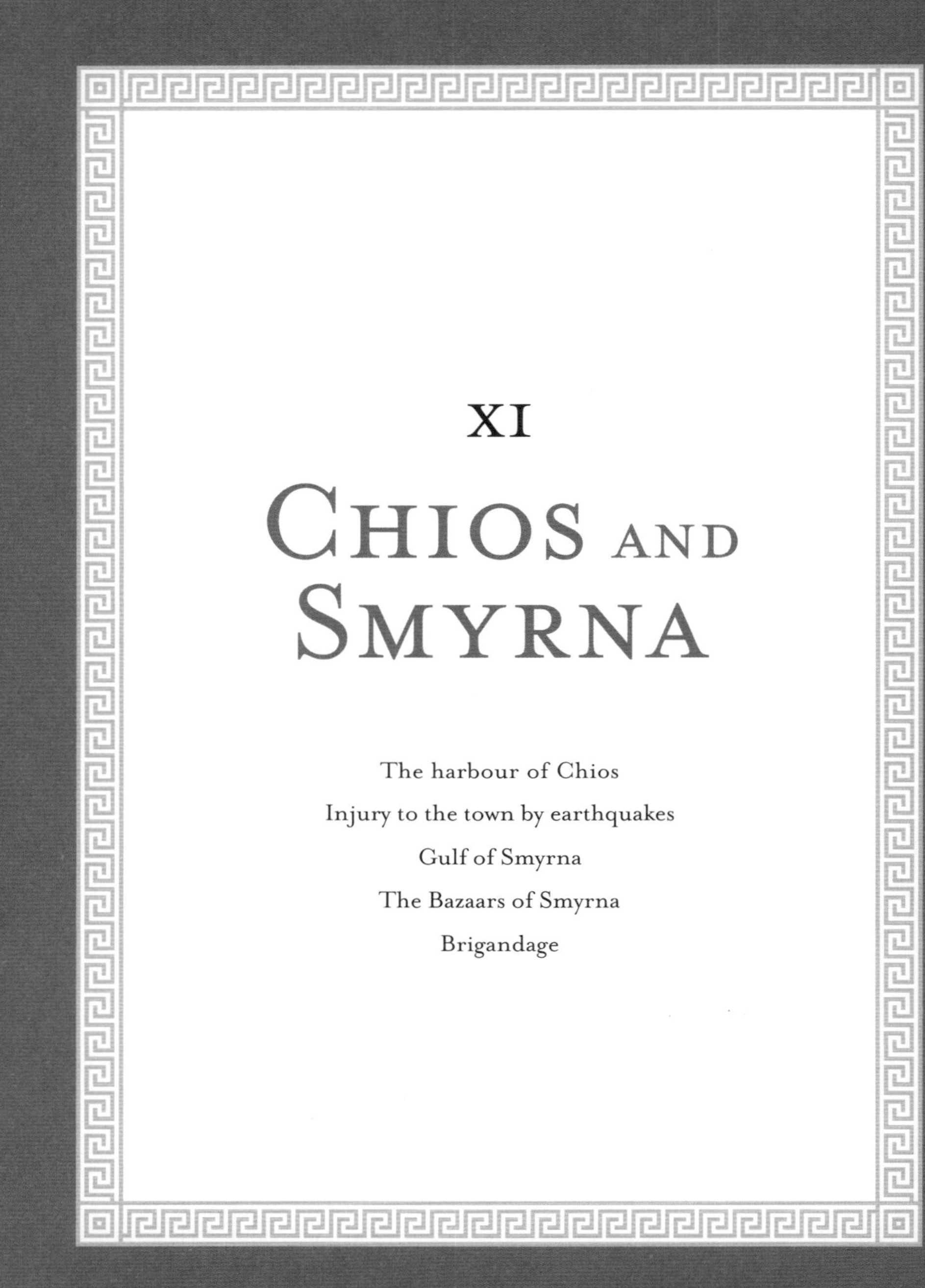

XI

Chios and Smyrna

The harbour of Chios

Injury to the town by earthquakes

Gulf of Smyrna

The Bazaars of Smyrna

Brigandage

On the morning of April 9th we left Patmos for Chios, passing close to the island of Samos, where we lay to for a moment off the port of Tigani. Although we heard tempting accounts of ancient ruins to be seen near Tigani we were afraid to land, as there was said to be fever in the island, and we did not like to risk the loss of our clean bill of health; so we took a look at the high, mountainous shores, and then steamed on to Chios. We reached Chios at about 5 p.m. and as we approached the harbour in the afternoon light we thought it the most beautiful island we had yet seen. The white town lies outspread along the bay, guarded by a ruined Genoese fortress on the water's edge—for Chios belonged to Genoa for nearly two hundred and fifty years—and behind it, stretching up to the enfolding mountains, is a veritable Conca d'Oro, a forest of orange-trees, cypresses, olives and figs. Here and there white country houses peep out through the verdure of delicious gardens, and even where we lay in the harbour the air was sweet with the smell of orange-blossoms.

We went ashore, and found the town a busy and dirty place. It has been entirely rebuilt since the great earthquake of 1881, and the dirty streets with tall houses and a pretentious French *Halle* are a poor substitute for the shady bazaars which they probably replaced. In spite of its loveliness a blight seems to hang over Chios, as if it had not recovered from the awful Turkish massacre which Canaris avenged by the destruction of the Turkish fleet, and which was followed in less than sixty years by the fresh disaster of the earthquake in which nearly six thousand perished. Chios has had more than her share of calamities, and the hopeless, degraded look of the place seems to say that the people are tired of fighting adversity. We wandered through the streets, looked at the stalls filled with queer, barbaric Chian pottery, and tried to see the fortress, but were stopped by a sentinel. It is curious that the Turks should imagine that strangers would take the trouble to carry off plans of their tumble-down forts, but we met with the same opposition everywhere in Turkish dominions. There must be beautiful rides all about Chios, but as the earthquake demolished every town and monastery in the island, there is no objective point to go to, and we were so much impressed with the desolation of the place that we were glad to start for Smyrna the next morning.

The 10th was a beautiful day with a cool breeze blowing, and when I came on deck rather late we were steaming up the wide gulf of Smyrna with our awnings set fore and aft. As we approached the head of the gulf the scenery grew very fine. The mountains rise boldly on every side, with a fringe of trees and meadows along the shore, and above the splendid harbour lies Smyrna, her white houses outspread upon the cypress-covered hills. As we entered the port crowded with shipping we thought that the quay with tall white houses and a tramway looked strangely European; and we were struck, as we had been at Chios, with the gabled, red-tiled roofs of the houses, which give a very un-Oriental look to the town, compared with the flat house-tops we had seen all through the Aegean.

The *Vanadis* was moored to the quay, and at 3 p.m. we went ashore, and went to the Ottoman Bank to call on Mr. Reade, one of the directors, to whom we brought letters. Mr. Reade kindly offered to take us through the bazaars, and we started down Frank Street, the principal street of Smyrna. It runs through the whole length of the Frank quarter, parallel with the quay, and is filled with European shops where everything is to be found which the civilized heart can desire. Connecting it with the other parallel streets and with the quay are long narrow passages with gates at either end, called "Frank passages," lined with houses, which were built and occupied by the Europeans at a time when the persecutions of the Turks made it necessary for them to have the means of shutting themselves in during any disturbance. These passages are now chiefly taken up with shops, restaurants, and wholesale ware-houses, but here and there the blossoming pergola of an old garden shows above a high wall.

Frank Street ends at the bazaars which, though less Oriental than those of Tunis, are bright and picturesque, and offer pretty pictures at every turn. The shops, however, are really small shops, with windows in the back, not mere niches as at Tunis, and the shop-keepers wear European dress and although they offer lemonade and coffee would probably be surprised if one accepted it. To make up for these disappointments, there are the trains of loaded camels, the donkeys with necklaces of large blue beads to protect them from the evil eye, the stalls hung with silks from Aleppo, the open spaces planted with blossoming acacias, the latticed fountains, the mosques with their fore-courts and minarets for the bazaars are a city in themselves, with khans, mosques, cafés, squares and fountains. Then there are the picturesque people: the Turkish women in brightly striped garments like dominos, with yellow shoes, and black veils over their faces; the Jewesses wearing long, loose robes of silk, with little caps embroidered in gold on their plaited hair, the gorgeous canvasses of the foreign consulates, in embroidered dresses, with sashes full of jeweled pistols and yataghans, the old Turks in flowing robes and white turbans, the lemonade-sellers in bright yellow coats, the negresses in gaudy colours, the gypsies, the Greek priests, all forming a medley of different types which I have never seen equalled anywhere.

Nothing, in fact, can be more curious than the mixture of Orientalism and European civilization which meets one at every turn in Smyrna. I could not get used to seeing the tramways blocked by trains of loaded camels, the *voitures-de-place* filled with veiled Turkish women, and the savage-looking Turks and Albanians with weapons in their belts, side by side with fashionably-dressed Levantines and Europeans. In Frank Street one can buy Zola's last novel, a ready-made dress, or a *batterie de cuisine*, while in the bazaars close by are sold narghilehs, clogs from Bagdad, *rahat-loukoum*, and other Eastern products. We stayed a long time in the bazaars, and on our return to the yacht we had a visit from Mr. Charles Biliotti (brother to our Rhodian friend) and his wife.

The next day was a very busy one, as coal and water were being put in, the boat's bottom scrubbed, and the men all fitted with straw hats. In the morning I went to call on Mme. Biliotti, and she took us all through the bazaars and showed us many things which we had failed to see the day before—such as the provision booths where bits of roasted meat are stuck on skewers all ready to be bought and eaten, the interior of the Khans, and the very curious iron-mongers' bazaar. We had a late luncheon on the yacht, and our fellow-traveller went for a drive in the suburbs, but we declined to peril our necks after the tales of brigandage which everyone in Smyrna had poured into our ears.

Mr. and Mrs. Emmett (the American consul and his wife) came to dine with us, and although they lived not far from the quay and were escorted by an armed cavass, they thought it unsafe to drive or walk, and therefore came from their house by boat. They told us the most appalling things about the state of Smyrna. It was considered unsafe to drive out in a carriage as far as the suburban villages of Bournabat and Boujah, where many of the Europeans have their summer villas, and within a month twenty one murders had been committed in the streets of Smyrna. Several rich merchants had received letters signed "One of the Seven," and threatening them with death if they refused to pay some thousands of francs. The first man who received such a letter disregarded it, and was murdered in the open day at his own door; consequently the next victims selected paid their tribute without a murmur. This state of affairs was said to be caused by the dishonesty of the governor of Smyrna, who had for some time past pocketed the salaries of the police, and left them no resource but to connive at the murders and robberies and take a share of the booty as their payment. As to the murderers themselves, the Turks all said they were Greeks, but in a cosmopolitan place like Smyrna it seems more likely that they were made up of the dregs of different nations.

Two years ago some of these brigands seized a young man, a cousin of Mme. Billiotti's, in the neighbourhood of Smyrna, and kept him captive for several weeks, ill-treating him cruelly. The sum they asked for his ransom was so large that his father, who was a poor man, could not pay it, and not until a collection was taken up throughout the city could the needed money be obtained. Shortly afterwards the police, who had probably received their salaries that month, caught the brigands, cut off their heads and carried them back to Smyrna, where they were impaled on the gates of the Governor's Palace.

WE LOOKED AT THE STALLS FILLED WITH QUEER,
BARBARIC CHIAN POTTERY.

XII

Mitylene

View from the Citadel

Damages by earthquake fully repaired

Mitylene, the most beautiful island of the Aegean

The Governor

A child of eight years who speaks five languages

Village of Morea

Marble chair of Potamon

Its age near two thousand years

We left Smyrna on the morning of the 12th, with the intention of running as far as we could towards the plains of Troy, but a violent storm of wind and rain drove us to take shelter in the harbour of Mitylene. At about 4 p.m. the weather cleared, and going on deck we looked out over the lovely bay, locked in softest hills, and fringed by groves of acacia, orange and fig, with scattered villas on the slopes about the town. Just then a large boat came alongside, rowed by Turkish sailors and flying the Turkish flag. It proved to be the Governor's private boat, and contained his dragoman, a Greek, who had come to put himself at our disposal during our stay at Mitylene. He spoke French, and a word or two of English, and wore a uniform; in fact he seemed more like an *aide-de-camp* than like the ordinary dragoman, who is merely an Eastern *valet-de-place*. We went ashore in the Governor's boat, and the dragoman took us through the town to a garden overgrown with roses, lemon-blossoms and yellow jasmine; then he led us up to the Citadel on the hill above the bay, first having obtained the Governor's permission that we should see it. The damage done by the great earthquake of twenty years ago has been carefully repaired, and the fortress is picturesque and well-preserved. Here and there I noticed slabs of marble encrusted in the walls with bas-reliefs upon them, some Greek, some Byzantine. The view from the battlements is incomparable, looking over the bay, the town backed by gardens of orange and olive, and enclosed in mountains, and, across the straits, to the neighbouring coast of Asia. In fact Mitylene is the most beautiful island of the Aegean. From end to end the country is a blossoming garden, and in the town the streets are shaded by cypress and olive-trees, or white acacias, which we found in full bloom, while a wealth of flowers pours over every garden-wall. We took a long walk with the dragoman, and after stopping at several houses to look at some pieces of embroidery, we went to pay our respects to the Governor. His Excellency Fahry Bey had already moved into his summer villa, a small yellow cottage built on a ridge overlooking the harbour and the Asian coast. In front of it is a terrace laid in black and white pebbles, overhanging the sea and shaded by a great plane-tree under whose branches a fountain falls into a square tank. On the edge of this terrace was placed a semi-circle of red velvet chairs, and as we approached the Governor and his *aide-de-camp* came forward to receive us. The dragoman, after performing a low salaam, presented us to his Excellency, who asked us to be seated and ordered some lemonade to be brought. Fahry Bey is a very agreeable man and speaks French fluently, having been Secretary of Legation in several European capitals, as well as Ambassador to Persia. He told us that his little boy, Ali Bey, a child of eight, who was riding up and down on a velocipede, under the trees, spoke five languages, Persian, Greek, Turkish, French and Italian. Fahry Bey was at some time Secretary of Foreign Affairs in the Turkish Cabinet, and we heard in Mitylene that a change of administration had sent him into a kind of exile as Governor of the island. He is doing great good there by building carriage-roads, clearing out the harbour, and maintaining such strict order among his subjects that it is said to be safe to walk alone about the island any time of the day or night. He expressed his disappointment that we had not entered the inner harbour, which he has just cleared of sand, and also that Madame Fahry was too ill to visit the yacht, which he himself promised to do the next day. He owns a small steam-yacht, or rather I believe it is owned by the Turkish Government; and the Captain was put at our disposal as pilot in case we wished to visit any other parts of the island.

The next morning at 9 a.m. our friend the dragoman again came on board the *Vanadis*, and we all went ashore and found a landau with a capital pair of horses awaiting us. It is the only carriage in the island except the governor's. We drove out to the large village of Morea, a drive of about an hour through the least pretty part of the island, and getting out of the carriage, walked through the village, which is dirty and bad-smelling, to an olive-grown valley where the famous Roman aqueduct stands. Its picturesque arches span the valley, which is enclosed in olive-covered hills and watered by a stream fringed with oleanders.

After lingering here for some time, we walked back to Morea, and stopped at a house belonging to an aunt of the dragoman, an old lady who received us with the usual friendliness of her people. The house itself was a tall tower called a *pyrgos* with only two rooms on each floor. We were taken into the chief room, which was painted light blue, with a long divan

THE FORTRESS IS PICTURESQUE AND WELL PRESERVED.

under the windows, and a fountain in the wall; and here an ancient handmaid served us with an elaborate banquet in several courses, consisting of quince marmalade and water, coffee, aquavitae, and *rahat-loukoum*.

The old lady then brought out some embroideries which she had worked in her youth, and which she showed with great pride. The embroideries of Mitylene have a decidedly Turkish look in colouring and design, especially the long towels worked at either end which the young girls formerly made and hung up in the best room of the *pyrgos* as specimens of their handiwork, and afterwards took with them as part of their dot. We bought several of these towels, which are now no longer made, from a man in Morea. The Turkish girls in Mitylene, we were told, still embroider and give their work to their sweethearts; but Greek work is very hard to get.

From Morea we drove back to the yacht, and in the afternoon Fahry Bey came on board with two *aides-de-camp* and his little boy. We mustered the crew and ran up a Turkish flag in honour of his visit, and sherry and candied fruits were solemnly consumed in the deck-house.

After he left we went ashore again to take another drive. This time we mounted the hill behind the town following one of the fine roads which Fahry Bey has built through an endless succession of olive-groves carpeted with white and pink cistus in full bloom. When we reached the yoke of the hill we had a fine view over the town and harbour of Mitylene in one direction, and in the other over the beautiful land-locked waters of Port Iero, enclosed in wooded hills. The road winds down the mountainside for some distance towards Port Iero, and is ultimately intended to reach the village of that name; but unfortunately such work is done in Turkey not by the Government but by the individual energy of the governors, and if, as is probable, Fahry Bey leaves here in a year or two the chances are that his successor will let all the roads in Mitylene go to rack and ruin.

On the way home we drove along another road which skirts the harbour, past neat country-houses in gardens of fig, pomegranate and rose; then we returned to the town, and went to see the Archbishop of Mitylene, from whom we wished to obtain a letter to the First Man of

Mount Athos. The Archbishop was away but his secretary afterwards sent us the letter, and in the courtyard of the modest archi-episcopal Palace, we saw the famous marble chair of Potamon the sophist, of which Newton speaks.

It is beautifully sculptured, with marble gryphons forming the arms, and a Greek inscription under the seat which runs as follows: "The place of honour of Potamon, son of Lesbonax."

According to Newton "this chair is probably from an ancient theatre, where Potamon must have sat in the front row among the civil and religious dignitaries of Mitylene. Potamon was, like his father, a sophist, and resided in Rome, where he gained the favour of the Emperor Tiberius." The chair therefore is nearly two thousand years old.

After this we went on board the yacht, and after dinner the dragoman came on board and brought us several farewell gifts, two earthenware vases roughly ornamented with flowers in relief, which are specimens of the modern pottery of Mitylene, and a large bottle of wine from his own vineyard, as well as a photograph of himself on which he had written "To remember of a friend at Mitylene."

THE INTERIOR OF THE CHURCH IS AT PRESENT COVERED WITH ARCHAIC LOOKING FRESCOES.

THE EFFECT IS RICH AND BRILLIANT.

WHITE WINDMILLS, RANGED LIKE SENTINELS AGAINST THE SKY.

THEN HE LED US UP TO THE CITADEL ON THE HILL ABOVE THE BAY.

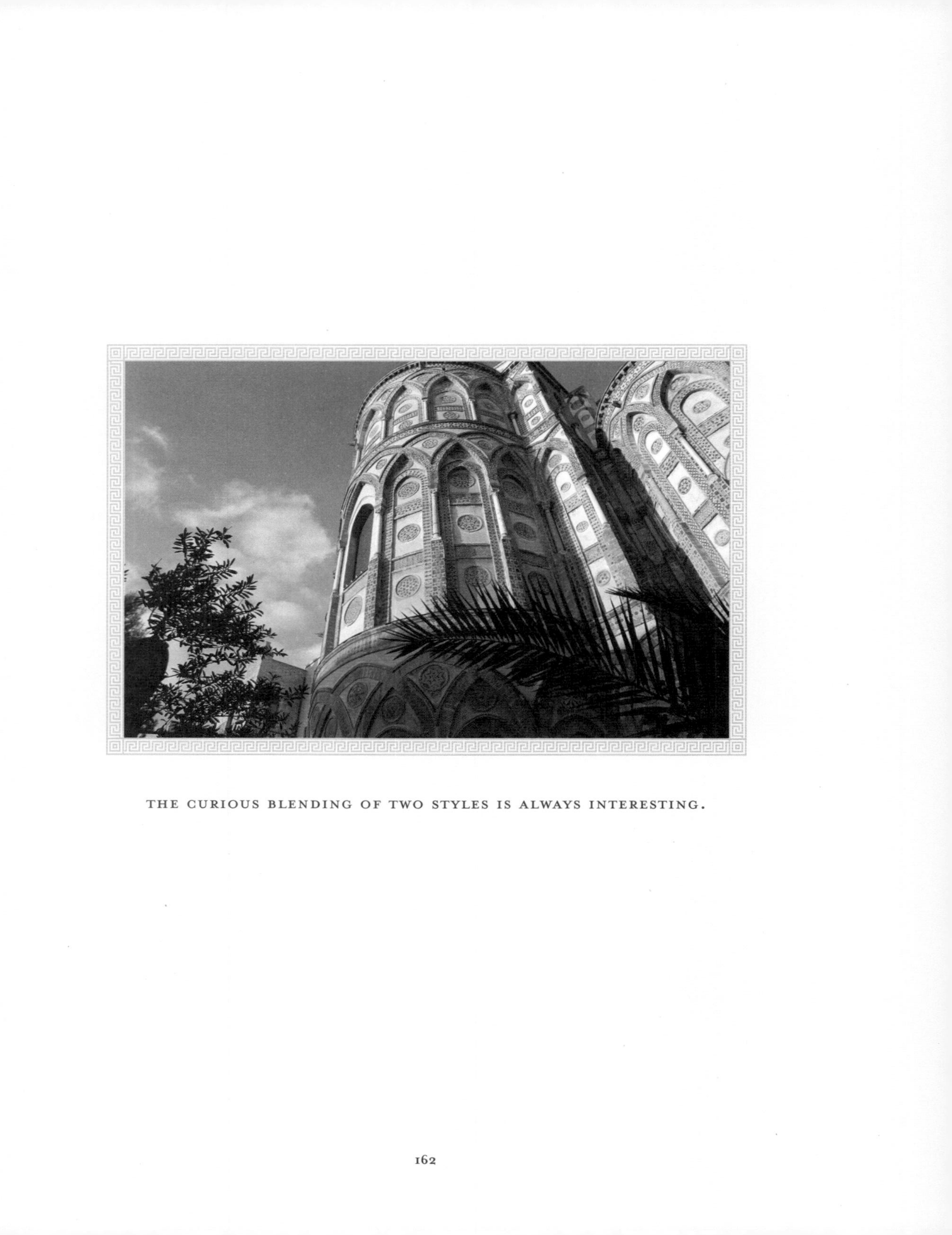

THE CURIOUS BLENDING OF TWO STYLES IS ALWAYS INTERESTING.

THE CLOISTER IS ENCLOSED IN A ROUND-ARCHED ARCADE.

WE FOUND ATHENS HAS THE NEAT, PROSPEROUS AIR OF A GERMAN REZI-DENZ, INCONGRUOUSLY OVERSHADOWED BY THE ACROPOLIS.

THE MARBLE HAS TAKEN A PRIMROSE HUE, NOW FADING TO IVORY.

THE LANDSCAPE, OVERHUNG BY A GREY SKY THROUGH WHICH THE SUN FAINTLY STRUGGLED, HAD AN UNREAL, MOONLIT LOOK.

WE WERE QUITE UNPREPARED FOR THE BEAUTY
OF THE APPROACH.

WE TRIED TO SEE THE FORTRESS, BUT WERE STOPPED BY A SENTINEL.

A STREAM FRINGED WITH OLEANDERS.

XIII

Mount Athos

Port Iero

History of Mount Athos

Two kinds of Monasteries

The Anchorites

Legends concerning the Peak of Athos

The author starts on a voyage of discovery and alarms the caloyers

Stavroniketa

This voyage ends at Pantacrotoras

The Turkish Governor wearied of *"rien que des masculins et pas de théâtre"*

Marvelous *eikons* and famous treasures of the monasteries

Xeropotamu

Xenophu, Dogheireiu, Costamunito and Russico

Arrival at Euripo

Admiral Mansell

We had intended to leave Mitylene at midnight on the 13th of April, but the weather changed in the night and by morning it was blowing a gale. The Captain thought that we could start, but the weather was so bad that we had to put back, and finally after some hesitation we decided to run around into Port Iero, but as I was not up I unluckily did not see the entrance to the port, which is said to be very fine, and is called I believe "the Little Bosphorus."

We anchored off a small cove with a group of villages on the hillside above it, but it was too rough to land, so we steamed to another anchorage on the opposite side of the bay, where the water was quieter. Here we went ashore, and walked through shady olive-groves to a village on a hill about a mile and a half from the shore. This village, though prettily situated, is dirty and unattractive, and, after picking our way through its muddy streets followed by the sullen stares of the inhabitants, we walked back to the yacht.

The wind fell that night and the next morning we started at 5 a.m. for Mount Athos. Although it was still cold the weather was beautiful and in spite of the recent gale the waves had subsided into a long soothing roll. We ran between the islands of Shati and Lemnos, and as we coasted along the western side of Lemnos, we caught sight of the peak of Athos rising faint and blue from the sea ahead of us. The nearer we drew the more beautiful it became, until at last its mighty wall was close before us, dark against the brilliant sky as the sun set in a yellow blaze behind the low hills of the Sithonian promontory.

It was ticklish work groping along in the dusk to find an anchorage on the east coast of the Sacred Mountain, but fortunately the night was calm, and the new moon helped us, as well as the fishing beacons which the monks had lighted along the water's edge, and by 8.30 p.m. we had anchored in a shallow bay about ten miles from the peak of Athos.

So little seems to be known about Mount Athos that a few words about its history may not be amiss. Tradition ascribes the founding of some of the monasteries to the time of Constantine, and it is likely that hermitages and colonies of monks existed there from an early time. Tozer, however, calls St. Athanasius of Trebizond the "originator of the present conventual system" on Mount Athos. He founded the Lavra in the tenth century. This name of course signifies "the street," and owes its origin to the street of cells which was the earliest form of monastery; and this goes to show that the Lavra when built, was the chief, if not the only monastery on the promontory. Others were soon built, and there are now about twenty on the sacred mountain, in addition to the central village of Karyes and the numerous outlying retreats and communities of farming monks. Tozer calls these monasteries "with the sole exception of Pompeii, the most ancient existing specimens of domestic architecture," and the fact that they are still used for the purpose for which they were originally intended, adds, of course, not a little to their interest.

The monasteries are all governed by a Superior called the "First Man of Athos;" but although Turkey allows great privileges to this ancient settlement of the Greek Church, a Turkish Governor lives at Kayres, who nominally represents the Sultan's suzerainty although his actual authority is of the slenderest.

The monasteries are of two kinds, the Coenobite, under the general rule of one Hegumenos, where the caloyers have "all things in common," and the Idiorrhythmic, where the caloyers, although living together, preserve a great measure of independence, take their meals apart, and even maintain their private servants if they choose.

It need hardly be added that the rule in the latter monasteries is much less strict, and more popular among the richer monks. The caloyers are nearly all laymen, as they have too many services to perform if they take holy orders. They are a rough and illiterate set, about three thousand in number, not including the Seculars who are employed as servants or farm-labourers without taking monastic vows. The monasteries are full of treasures in the shape of reliquaries, crosses, *eikons* and frescoes; in fact the churches of Mount Athos are said to contain the finest collection of medieval jewelry in Europe.

In some of the monasteries all the monks are Greek, in others Slavonic and Russian; and Russico, the Russian monastery, is said to be in the present day a hot-bed of Russian political spies. This possibility, and the telegraph-wire which has recently been carried to the village of

Karyes, are the only discordant elements in the curiously preserved mediaevalism of the Sacred Mountain. Otherwise the life there is as archaic as the frescoes on the chapel walls.

Besides the monasteries there are the hermitages, built in the clefts of the peak of Athos, where anchorites live in seclusion as complete as that of the Thebaid; to say nothing of the Sketes, or villages of farming monks gathered around a central church.

The early established rule that no female, human or animal, is to set foot on the promontory, is maintained as strictly as ever; and as hens fall under this ban, the eggs for the monastic tables have to be brought all the way from Lemnos.

As to the Sacred Mountain itself it is a narrow mountain or promontory about forty miles long, projecting into the sea from the coast-line of European Turkey. At the isthmus, where the ground is low, it is about a mile and a half wide; from this point it widens slightly and swells into a high ridge with variously broken slopes, rising as it runs seaward to a height of four thousand feet; then, after a slight drop in the land, the peak of Athos springs up suddenly almost seven thousand feet high, its summit crowned by the chapel of the Transfiguration, its base plunged in the Mediterranean waves.

Various legends are connected with the peak of Athos. It is said to have been the mountain on which Satan tempted Christ; and certainly from its peak one may well behold the riches and the glory of this world. Another story tells that St. Athanasius found a heathen image (probably a statue of Zeus) where the chapel now stands; and that the Devil punished him for throwing the idol into the sea by pulling down each night the rising walls of the Lavra.

On the 6th of August the festival of the Transfiguration is celebrated on the summit of the peak. The service goes on all night, at dawn the Eucharist is celebrated; and then the monks, marching in companies and chanting psalms, go down from the mountain to the monasteries below.

The next morning we looked out on a scene of exquisite beauty. I can only compare the promontory of the Sacred Mountain to one of the wooded mountain-spurs on the Italian side of a Swiss pass, torn up from its roots and plunged into the Mediterranean. We lay just off the monastery of Iveron, which stands on the water's edge, backed by hills covered from top to base with spring foliage, in which the brilliant pink of the blossoming Judas-trees was mingled with a hundred tints of green. Southward, the wooded slopes trend away towards the peak of Athos, its grey sides streaked with snowy marble, while to the north the indented shore-line carries the eye onward to the monasteries of Stavroniketa and Pantacrotoras on successive ledges of rock overhanging the sea. Iveron itself is a large building with mighty walls surmounted by a range of balconied wooden structures with steep tiled roofs, which produce the effect of a line of Swiss châlets perched on the top of a mediaeval fortress. A square gate-tower guards it at the water's edge, and above the gabled roofs rises a medley of cupolas and towers, backed by a mass of verdure.

High up the hillside the white walls of farm-houses and "Retreats" sparkle through thickets of larch, chestnut and plane-tree, and a few miles away, below the central ridge of the promontory, the roofs and steeples of the village of Karyes rise from a sea of bright foliage mixed with dark clumps of cypress.

At 9 a.m. the two men went ashore, taking the cook as interpreter, and set out for Karyes, where our books told us that the "First Man" lived. They had their walk for nothing, however, for when they got to Karyes they were told that to find the "First Man" they must go to the monastery of Vatopedi.

In the meantime I ordered steam up in the launch, and started out on a voyage of discovery, determined to go as near the forbidden shores as I could. I ran in close to Iveron and tried to photograph it, but the launch rolled so that I could not steady the camera. I then ran close in under the shore in the direction of Stavroniketa, passing a picturesque square tower used as a boathouse, with a fishing-boat drawn up under its dark archway. This tower is connected with the hillside by a wooden bridge close to which, in a bower of green, is perched a balconied cottage where a group of caloyers sat in the sunshine watching me with evident curiosity. We went in so close to the shore that they clambered hurriedly down the hill to prevent my landing, and with their shocks of black hair and long woolen robes flying behind them they were a wild enough looking set to frighten any intruder away.

Stavroniketa is a small but picturesque building on top of a rock which projects boldly into the sea. It is guarded by a gate-tower with an embattled parapet, and the stone arches of an aqueduct connect it with the hill behind. As we came close to it, I noticed that the rock on which it is built was thickly tufted with crimson snapdragon, white iris, and a sort of dwarf white-yellow laburnum.

As we steamed on the scene increased in beauty. Here a white chapel with a cross above its tiled cupola gleams through the trees; there a boat-house guarded by a tower stands close upon the shore; while scattered along the higher ridges of the promontory clusters of quaint houses with a minaret-like spire rising in their midst show the position of some *Skete* or independent community of farming monks. Where the slopes are not covered with foliage, they are terraced and planted with olives, vines and vegetables, and this careful tilth, combined with the trains of fat mules with pack-saddles grazing near the monasteries, gives a look of rural prosperity to the scene which is more suggestive of Switzerland or Tyrol than of the East.

We ran on to Pantacrotoras, which is placed close to the sea, like the others, and has a boat-harbour guarded by a rock on the top of which a large wooden cross has been fixed. A soft and fertile valley opens behind it in folds of richest green. From Pantacrotoras I turned and went back to the yacht, where the two men did not arrive until 3 p.m.

They brought with them the Turkish Governor of Mount Athos, who lives at Karyes, a stout old gentleman in frock-coat, fez and Rhodian boots, accompanied by a bristling little *aide-de-camp*. The Governor had brought me two old Turkish water jars of brown glazed pottery, which he called *"des antiques."* He was very jolly, and told me in the strangest possible French that he had been pining for two years on Mount Athos *"avec rien que des masculins et pas de théâtre."*

I think, however, that the motion of the yacht disturbed him, for he and his aide took leave rather hurriedly, becoming terribly involved with their large swords as they climbed down the side ladder to the gig.

WE GOT UNDERWEIGH AND STEAMED NORTHWARD ALONG THE COAST.

As soon as they had left we got underweigh and steamed northward along the coast of the monastery of Vatopedi, the wealthiest of the Sacred Mountain, and the largest except the Lavra. Its situation is less fine than that of the others, as Athos itself is out of sight, but it lies on a pretty bay enclosed in wooded hills, and forms in itself the finest group of buildings that we saw on the promontory.

A kind of terrace planted with olives and cypresses slopes gradually up from the beach to the base of the monastery-wall, and above this wall rises a fantastic line of balconies, towers, cupolas, tiled roofs and chimneys, interspersed here and there with slender bright green poplars. All these broken and irregular groups of buildings are painted in various colours, the châlets red, blue and green, and the towers white, while the roofs are covered with a lichenous growth like gold; and nothing can be conceived more brilliant and fairy-like than this combination of colours, lit up, as we saw it, by the setting sun, and framed in thickets of green.

Everything at Vatopedi is kept in perfect repair, and as all restorations at Mount Athos are made scrupulously like the original, one can admire the neatness and brightness of this great group of buildings without feeling that it involves the loss of anything that might have been better worth seeing.

Along the shore is a row of boat-houses (boat-towers would be more correct) each surmounted by its white châlet with black wooden balconies, and there are one or two stone outbuildings among the olives on the terraces.

I stayed on deck while the two men went ashore to visit the First Man, and no sooner had we anchored than the numberless balconies above the monastery-wall were crowded with caloyers gazing eagerly out at the yacht.

As I looked at this scene, it seemed hard to realize that many of the monasteries on the promontory have existed as we now see them since the tenth century, if not earlier, and that within their walls the same life has been going on unbroken—a life unaffected by modern inventions, discoveries and revolutions, a life as primly mediaeval as when the hermit Athanasius laid the first stone of the Lavra.

The two men were received with great courtesy wherever they went, and saw all the marvelous *eikons* set with uncut rubies, sapphires and emeralds, and the other famous treasures which the monasteries contain. In one of the monasteries they saw a monk frescoing a wall, and on going close to him they found that he was referring as he painted to the book of rules which was written for the artists of the Greek Church in the very beginning of Byzantine art by Dionysius of Agrapha. When they returned from Vatopedi they brought a picture of the monastery, which the First Man had given them, and also a boat-load of fresh vegetables contributed by the kindly monks.

No wonder that Xerxes cut a canal through the promontory of the Sacred Mountain, if the sea around it in his days was as lumpy and disagreeable as it was the next morning when we left Vatopedi.

There was a breeze from the eastward, and the strong current, racing against it, kicked up such a swell that even the flower vases on the swinging tables were upset, and everything around them drenched and damaged by the overflow.

We left Vatopedi at 9 a.m. and as there was too much sea on to stop at the Lavra we ran straight around Mount Athos to get in the lee of the west coast. When I came on deck we had just rounded the great peak, and were running close under it. On the western side it plunges down into the sea with splendid abruptness, its grey marble sides clothed far up with pine-trees "fledging the wild-ridged mountain steep by steep."

The water here is so deep that we ran in almost close enough, it seemed, to touch the cliffs, and as we drew near we saw that here and there, among the inaccessible ledges high overhead, hermitages clung like birds' nests to the rocks. In some cases they are no more than little wooden sheds, with balconies which literally overhang the precipitous cliffs; in others a tiny patch of ground has been reclaimed and a white hut peeps out through olives and Judas-trees.

How these places were ever reached, or how the hermits ever carried enough materials down the perpendicular face of the rock to build even such tiny hovels, is incomprehensible; but there they are, in every crack and cranny, and as we blew our whistle in passing a hermit appeared on each balcony with the promptitude of cuckoos in Swiss clocks when the hour strikes.

As we advanced the cliffs, though still four thousand feet high and very steep, were clothed in a thick scrub of cytisus, heather, Judas-trees and evergreen shrubs, mingled with olive and cypress, and to the sides of this green precipice clung two *Sketes*, more like Swiss villages than Greek monastic settlements. Their white houses, with the inevitable black balconies, showed pleasantly through the masses of spring foliage, presided over by the guardian spire of the central church, and I have never seen a lovelier picture of sunny peacefulness than they presented as we looked up at them from the deck of the yacht.

On we steamed and rounding a projecting point came suddenly upon the monastery of St. Paul, which Curzon well compares to a Gothic castle. With its towers backed by a crenellated wall it stands in bold picturesqueness at the foot of a mountain-chasm down which a torrent pours, as it seems, from the very peak of Athos. This stream had not yet begun to flow when we saw it, and masses of snow choked the upper part of its bed, contrasting strangely with the verdure below.

Nothing can be conceived finer than the scenery on this side of Athos. Two other monasteries follow in succession along the shore, each guarded in the rear by an embrasured wall, each with diversely grouped balconies, domes and towers, and a setting of many-tinted green. These are the monasteries of St. Dionysios and St. Gregory.

A little further on, perched on a splinter of rock which rises up hundreds of feet from the sea, stands the monastery of Simopetra, perhaps more grandly placed than any of the others. Seven tiers of balconies overhang its walls and an aqueduct with a double row of arches connects it with the face of the cliff behind.

Beyond this another bend of the coast took us out of sight of Athos, and the cliffs here become lower and less wild in aspect.

We passed Xeropotamu on a high cornice of rock, with its boathouse on a beach of white pebbles far below; then came Russico close to the water's edge, a large and ugly mass of buildings surmounted by bubble-like pale green domes on every one of which glitters a gilded cross.

After Russico comes the smaller and prettier Xenophu, also close to the water, with its square tower crowned by a peaked green roof, and close to this Dogheiareiu, a group of castellated walls and towers, with red domes and a clump of velvety cypresses.

We ran on a little further, catching sight of Constamunito high up the mountainside further to the north; then we turned, and steamed back to Russico, which owing to Tozer's bad map we had mistaken for Xeropotamu. At Russico an occasional steamer touches, and we tied up to a buoy while the two men went ashore.

They found a caloyer who spoke English and took them all over the monastery, but there was not much to be seen except the cross-shaped refectory frescoed with scenes from the life of Christ, where the monks sat eating while one of their number read aloud to them from a lectern in the wall. Each monk had a plate of soup, a lump of coarse bread and a handful of raw onions, and at every second plate there was a bottle of wine.

From Russico we steamed to Xeropotamu, which the men also wished to visit, and then back again to Russico, where we tied up to the buoy until it should be time to get underweigh for Euboea, as we did not wish to make the island of Skiathos before daylight.

We had a beautiful sunset, and a calm night flooded with moonlight which idealized the pale green domes of Russico; and at 10 p.m. we got underweigh, sadly remembering that henceforward we were homeward bound, and that each day would leave the "purple East" further in our wake.

At 4.30 the next morning we passed Skiathos, and entered the narrow channel between Greece and Euboea. It was very pretty winding down the quiet waters with the barren hills of Greece on one side, on the other those of Euboea, covered near the base with a low growth of light green conifers (probably the Isthmian pine) while the snow still lay thick upon the higher peaks.

During the day we passed an English steam-yacht of our own size, the first we had seen in a month, so far off the beaten track had our wanderings taken us.

As we advanced the hills seemed to close in around us, until at last it appeared as though we were sailing over a glassy inland lake, with the

LOOKING UP AT THE SHEER CLIFF ABOVE US WE SAW FAR, FAR OVERHEAD A WHITE MONASTERY.

walled town of Euripo lying at its head. As we approached we saw the drawbridge and fortress which connect Euripo with the mainland, and the narrow channel between them did not look wide enough to let a row-boat pass. The extraordinary current which runs here had set the wrong way just before we arrived, and we could not pass the bridge and run along, as we had hoped to do, as far as Armyra bay or Marathon. Our time was growing short, and we were realizing its value more and more each day, so that the delay was disappointing; but there was nothing to do but anchor, and spend the afternoon in exploring Euripo.

We rowed ashore expecting to land in five minutes as we usually did, but the officials were very disagreeable and kept us waiting a full hour for pratique. The inhabitants of Euripo are a sullen, ill-favored lot, and as for the town, a short walk sufficed to convince us that it has nothing to recommend it but its fine double girdle of walls and the fortress in the middle of the channel. We walked across the drawbridge, and under the arched gate of the fortress, which Mark guards; then over another small bridge to the mainland, where we took our first steps on the soil of Greece.

From thence the view over the town is pretty, although disfigured by factory chimneys; but when we walked through the streets we were much disappointed. I suppose that the frequent earthquakes are the cause of the shabby, tumble-down look of the houses, which are forlorn without being picturesque. We strolled about for a little while, and then hurried back to the drawbridge to see the yacht pass through with the change of the current. She looked like a picture as she shot through the narrow passage just beneath us, her awning set, her brasses shining in the sun, and rounded up to anchor in the bay beyond the bridge where we were to lie that night.

We were still loitering there, and I had just remarked that I could not understand what had induced the Englishman Captain Mansell, of whom Lady Brassey speaks, to fix upon Euripo as his place of abode, when a little old gentleman with a white beard came up to us and introduced himself as Admiral Mansell!

The ten or twelve years elapsing since Lady Brassey wrote, although they had brought him promotion, had apparently not shaken his allegiance to Euripo, for there he was, as ready as ever to take us to his house and offer us a bouquet from his garden, just as he is described as doing in *Sunshine and Storm*. He told us that at one time the hills of Attica on the further side of the drawbridge were so full of brigands that for eight months at a time he did not venture off the island; and on one occasion forty brigands marched into the town, surrounded the house of a Greek gentleman and carried him and his wife off for a six week's retreat among the mountains, from which they were only released by the payment of £2000. Since the murder of Messers Herbert and Vyner, however, there has been no brigandage in Greece, and except on the orders of Turkey or Albania the traveller is as safe as in Switzerland or Italy.

Admiral Mansell took us to his house, and showed us his garden full of orange and lemon trees, and the little one-story cottage in one corner where he and his wife sleep every night for fear of earthquakes. We asked him to dine with us but his wife was too ill for him to leave her, and so we wished him goodbye and returned to the yacht.

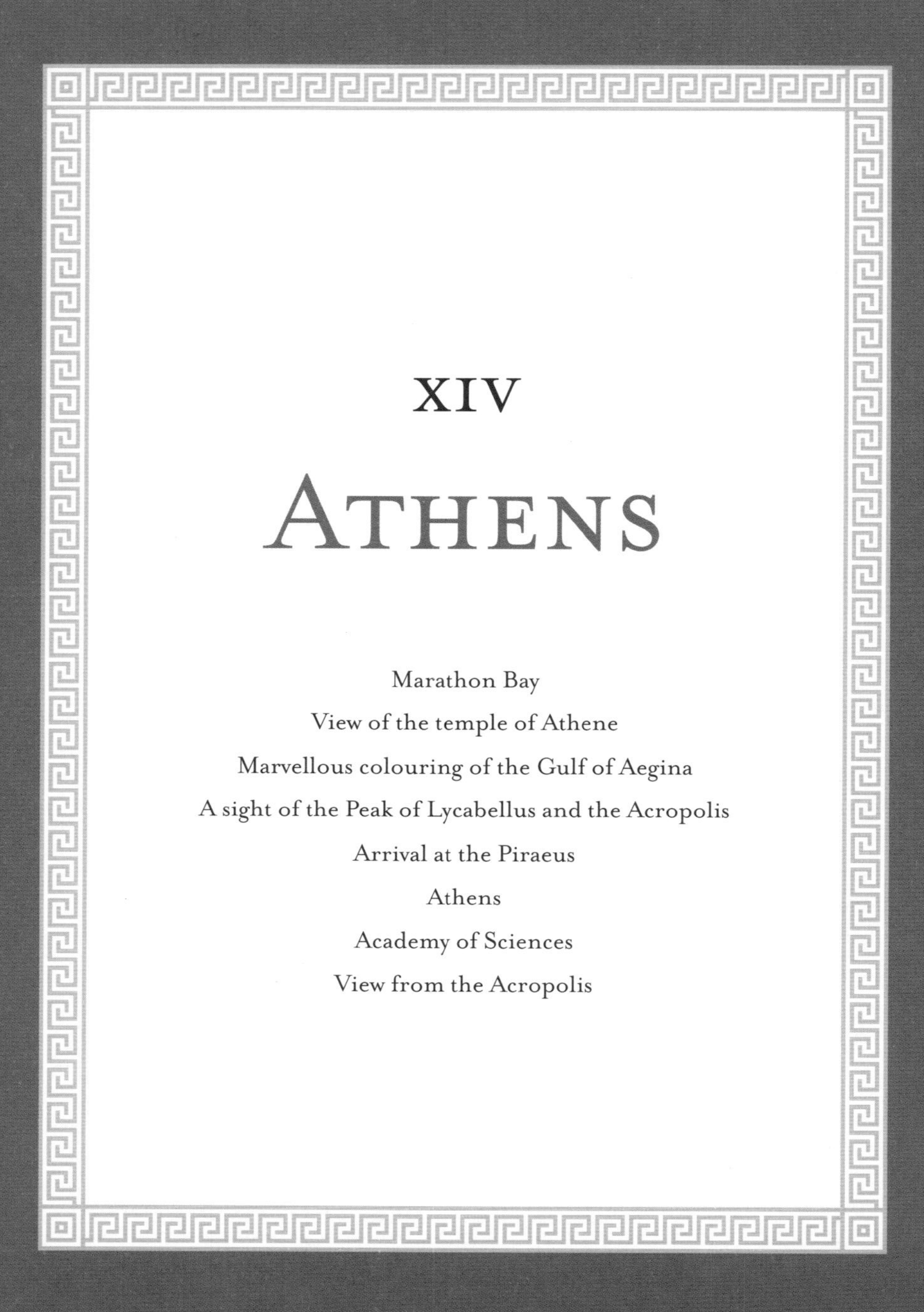

XIV

Athens

Marathon Bay

View of the temple of Athene

Marvellous colouring of the Gulf of Aegina

A sight of the Peak of Lycabellus and the Acropolis

Arrival at the Piraeus

Athens

Academy of Sciences

View from the Acropolis

On the morning of the 19th of April at 5 o'clock we started from Euripo for the Peiraeus. When I came on deck we were just entering Marathon bay, a lovely sheet of water enclosed in soft hills, with the long crescent-shaped plain where the battle was fought lying at their base. The hills are bare, but the plain is studded with large trees, either olives or caroubas, and at one point there is a fine grove of umbrella-pines along the shore.

We lay to long enough to discover the mound near the beach, under which the dead Greeks were buried; then we steamed out again and continued on our course down the channel of Euboea.

We passed between the island of Makronisi and the low, desolate hills of the mainland, beneath which the sea-shore is disfigured by several factories, and soon after we caught sight of the white columns of the temple of Athene on the steep cliff of Sunium. From this point the scenery is exquisite. For a long time after rounding Sunium we saw the gleaming marble of the ruined temple, which at this point seems to dominate the whole scene; then we entered the gulf of Aegina, and new beauties unfolded themselves before us. I had always imagined that there was a good deal of exaggeration in the enthusiasm of different writers over the effect of light on the Greek hills, but I am now convinced that they rather understate the truth. Never in my life have I seen such a marvellous scale of colours as clothes the Gulf of Aegina; first the blinding blue sea, then the rocks projecting into it, brilliant with tints of russet and primrose and streaks of pale green; then the hills of the middle distance, of tenderest ashes-of-roses, with blue cloud-shadows flecking their slopes, lastly the sapphire-blue of the remoter mountains, melting imperceptibly into the embracing sea and sky. When one considers that this rainbow of colours is made up without the help of a single tree, or even a blade of grass, it is indeed a thing to wonder at.

Presently we passed Aegina, and looking up the bay ahead of us I saw across an intervening slope, which happened to be in shadow, a high sunlit rock with a chapel on its top—the peak of Lycabettus. I looked again, and a little further on was another rock, like a huge platform of sil-

THE KING'S PALACE IS NOT A THING OF BEAUTY, BUT BEHIND IT ARE GARDENS OF ENCHANTING LOVELINESS.

THE ROUND BASIN HEDGED BY TALL PAPYRUS.

ver, crowned by a range of silvery colonnades, and relieved against an ethereal background of sapphire mountains.

Thus the Acropolis rose before us—

"A city such as visions
Build from the purple crags and silver towers
Of battlemented clouds"

—And never afterwards did it seem so beautiful.

Soon the white houses of Athens appeared in the plain below, with a fringe of olive orchards and a frame of surrounding hills.

We anchored in the crowded Piraeus at about 6 p.m. and took the 6.30 train to Athens. On arriving there, a long drive through the busy Hermes Street brought us to Palace Square, at the upper end of which stands the huge white Palace of King George. Palace Square is lined by hotels, in the largest of which, the Hotel de la Grande-Bretagne, our rooms were engaged.

We found Athens a white, glaring town, with wide avenues shaded with pepper-trees, handsome houses with gardens in front, good shops, restaurants, cab-stands, a band of music playing in the square—in short it has the neat, prosperous air of a German Residenz, incongruously overshadowed by the Acropolis.

The King's Palace is not a thing of beauty, but behind it are gardens of enchanting loveliness, which are generously opened to the public every afternoon, and where one may walk for hours under trees garlanded in red and pink roses, and trellises of Banksias and yellow Jasmine, or between hedges of blossoming laurustinus twenty or thirty feet high.

Among the modern buildings of Athens there is, however, one of undoubted interest, and that is the Academy of Sciences, built by a rich Greek banker of Vienna. It is an attempt, and I think a successful one, to reproduce a Greek building of the Ionic order. The marble is toned to soft ivory colour, the volutes of the capitals are picked out with gold, and the sculptures of the pediments are relieved against a blue background. Whatever its faults may be, I think it shows how perfectly suited Greek architecture was to the Greek climate and landscape, and how grotesque are the classic reproductions in northern countries, with their smoke-blackened columns and weather-beaten sculptures.

It is interesting to go to the Acropolis from this building, carrying its colour in one's eye, and to invest the sunburnt ruins of the Parthenon and the Erectheum with the tints which must once have belonged to them. And yet perhaps they are more beautiful as they are. The marble has taken a primrose hue, now fading to ivory, now deepening to russet, and the columns absolutely glow in the sunshine against the blue sky.

On every side the view is exquisite. The eye ranges from Hymettus and Lycabettus to the gulf of Eleusis, the islands of Psyttaleia and Salamis, and the blue mountains of Aegina. In the plain below lie the groves of Colonus and the Academy; in the foreground rises the rock of Areopagus. Far below, on one side, the Theseum lifts its unbroken range of pillars, looking in its wonderful preservation like a toy model of the temple, on the other side the golden-brown columns of Jupiter Olympius stand picturesquely clustered among their fallen fellows.

But even lovelier is the scene on such a full-moon night as we had, when the temples seem made of ivory, and far beneath lies Athens, twinkling with hundreds of lights, with shadowy clumps of trees rising between the house-roofs, and a misty wall of mountains all around.

Whatever else of interest Athens contains is so subordinated to the Acropolis, that it is after all but a perfunctory glance one casts at the sculpture of the theatre of Dionysius, the exquisite columns of the Choragic Monument of Lysicrates, or even the treasures of the Museums. So at least we found it, and while we were in Athens each afternoon drew us back to the Acropolis, and curtailed our chances of more exhaustive sight-seeing. Even the Byzantine churches, which I knew to be interesting, which elsewhere I should have journeyed far to see, held me only a moment as I hurried back to the Acropolis. Perhaps on a second visit to Athens one might recover one's sense of proportion; I hope some day to find out.

XV

The Ionian Islands

The *Vanadis* proceeds to Corinth and the travellers join her by train

Bay of Eleusis

Canal across the Isthmus

Departure for Argostoli

Mills worked by sea water

The village of Samos on Cephalonia, one of the loveliest of the Ionian Islands

The island of Ithaca

Vathy

Gulf of Molo

Arrival at Corfu

Greek Palm Sunday

Splendid dresses of the women

A beautiful procession

Meanwhile the *Vanadis*, after lying at the Piraeus long enough to take in coal and have some painting done, had proceeded on her way to Corinth, and on the morning of April 24th at 6.30 we started from Athens to join her by train. Our Minister to Greece, Mr. Fearn, went with us, intending to leave the yacht at Corfu, where he was to take leave of the King before going away for a few months' holiday.

The line from Athens to Corinth runs past the groves of Colonus and Academy, and across the stony bed of the Kephissus, and the landscape looked very pretty in the early light, with the peasants in their white dresses and scarlet aprons at work among the olive-shaded wheat fields. Very picturesque are the white linen gowns of the women, their embroidered white cloth overcoats and red sashes and aprons, but they are rivaled by the men in white fustanellas and braided jackets, with rough frieze or sheepskin capotes.

We ran along the lovely bay of Eleusis, and past Megara, through thickets of the feathery Isthmian pine, with the sea close under us, and beautiful glimpses of Salamis and Psyttaleia in the distance. Presently we came to the canal which is being cut across the Isthmus, and as we passed over it on a bridge we looked down and saw hundreds of men at work between the steep embankments below. I believe that the Canal is to be opened next year.

At 11.30 we reached Corinth, where the yacht awaited us, and as we got underweigh we had a fine view of the snow peak of Parnassus; but on the whole the sail down the gulf disappointed us, perhaps because the day was overcast and windy. The scenery, however, grew finer as we approached the so-called "little Dardanelles" just above Patras. There were rumours of small-pox in Patras, so we anchored in a bay to the south of it, and started the next morning at daybreak for Argostoli in Cephalonia.

A strong southeast wind was blowing after us, and a good tossing we had from the time we left the Gulf of Corinth until we got under the lee of the island of Cephalonia.

We reached Argostoli at 12 o'clock, and after luncheon we went ashore. The situation of Argostoli is not as pretty as that of many other towns in this part of the world, but the soft russet-tinted mountains just opposite, on the other side of the bay, are very beautiful. They are almost bare of foliage, and the russet-tinge is produced by patches of cultivated soil where the currant vine is grown.

We walked through the long, clean street of the town, but finding that we ourselves were the only objects of interest that it contained (at least to judge from the behaviour of the inhabitants) we sent for a carriage and started to see the famous mills worked by sea-water. We were lucky enough to find a good barouche with an excellent pair of horses, and were soon bowling along to the mills, while the *Vanadis* steamed out of the harbour, with orders to wait for us at Samos on the east coast of the island.

A drive of ten minutes along the shore brought us to the mills, one of which, however, is no longer working. We went into the other, and although natural phenomena are generally a fraud, it was certainly curious to see the current rushing in from the sea, turning the wheel, and disappearing in a rocky field a few yards beyond the mill.

Having watched it for some time, we returned to the carriage and started on our drive across the island, with many doubts as to the possibility of reaching Samos before night-fall.

We drove through Argostoli again, and crossed the head of the bay by a long bridge and causeway built, of course, like every other good road in the Ionian Islands, under the English administration. Beyond this the road winds up the hillside and, passing through a wooded gorge, we came out upon a wide valley enclosed in many-tinted hills. The whole of this valley is planted with currant vineyards, whose bright green foliage is shaded by the giant olive-trees for which Cephalonia is famous. We drove through these vineyards to the further side of the valley, and then started on another long climb up the mountains. The views looking back from this ascent are very beautiful, and the hillsides, where they are not cultivated, are covered with a low growth of cistus, heath, and blazing yellow cytisus. As we mounted higher, we passed clumps of hawthorn in full bloom, which perfumed all the air; then we reached a colder region, where the currant vines were just putting out their first leaves, and here the patches of red soil produced the umber colouring which we had seen from below on entering the port of Argostoli.

At length we reached the yoke of the mountains and descended into another valley, higher and less fertile, with the Monastery of St. Gerasimo lying some distance off on our right, and the pine-covered peak of the Black Mountain towering up ahead of us. A road built by Sir Charles Napier, to whom in fact Cephalonia owes all her roads, leads up to the top of the Black Mountain, nearly 6000 feet above the sea, whence there is a splendid view over all the Ionian Islands and the mountains of Greece.

We left the Black Mountain on our right, and after another short climb drove rapidly down, skirting the edge of a wild ravine with the bed of a mountain stream in its depths. Presently a turn in the road showed us the wooded valley of Samos, with the cliffs of Ithaca rising, as it seemed, a stone's throw off across the sapphire straits, and from here it was a lovely drive down through the olives to the village of Samos on the shore.

We got there safely at sunset, in spite of all the warnings about the length of the way which we had received at Argostoli; but strange to say the yacht was not in sight.

We wandered about a little while on the beach, and then went to the village inn, where we found a wide balcony overhanging a garden full of roses and blossoming lemon-trees. Here we were served with a supper of macaroni, cheese and "sweet wine," while the full-moon, rising above the hills behind us, poured its light over the quiet waters of the bay and through the leafy pergola above our heads. Lovely as it was, we were beginning to grow rather anxious about the *Vanadis* when at 10 p.m. we saw her lights at the mouth of the harbour; and not the least pleasant part of the day was the quick pull out to her in the gig across the moonlit water. We found that she had met a very heavy sea outside, and this had delayed her unexpectedly.

We lay at Samos that night, and if we had been able to spare the time we could have passed another day or two delightfully in Cephalonia, which is one of the loveliest of the Ionian Islands, and has both classic and Byzantine ruins to show, as well as charming drives in all directions. Time was flying, however, and at 8 the next morning we steamed across the straits to Vathy in the island of Ithaca.

As we entered the blue bay of Molo it seemed impossible that a harbour should be concealed anywhere among the folds of the surrounding hills; but suddenly we rounded a green point and found ourselves in the port of Vathy.

At its entrance lies a little rocky island, and further in is another, wholly covered by a low white building which rises picturesquely out of the water, but is used for the unromantic purpose of a prison.

The town itself slopes up a hillside from the water's edge in terrace-like lines; and in front of one of the houses on the quay we saw a great black ship, drawing twelve or fifteen feet of water, moored to the shore in the manner so often described in accounts of port Vathy.

We went ashore, and an old Maltese, who had been a sailor in the English navy and who told us that he received a small pension from the English government, offered to show us the sights of Vathy. He led us up the hill behind the town to the English cemetery, a tiny walled space, containing a few graves overgrown with huge rosebushes in full bloom; then he showed us the church near by, and took us through the streets of the forlorn little town. I have never seen greater appearances of misery and poverty than in Ithaca, but the people were uniformly kind and courteous, and many of them, as I passed through the streets, stepped from their doors to hand me bunches of roses and lemon-blossoms.

We said goodbye to our old guide, who pathetically begged us for a little "good English tea," which we sent him in the afternoon; and after lunching on the yacht we went ashore again and started at once for a drive.

We skirted the shores of the gulf of Molo, following the edge of two little bays overshadowed with huge olive-trees which actually leaned their branches over the water; it is under these trees that Ulysses is supposed to have lain when the Phaeacians landed him on the shores of Ithaca. Such at least is Stillman's theory, although tradition places the cave of Ulysses on the other side of the island. Beyond this the road—an English legacy, of course—mounts a hill to the foot of Mount Aetos, on whose top stand the Cyclopean walls called the Castle of Ulysses. It was too warm to climb to the top of Aetos, so we sat awhile enjoying the beautiful view looking westward across the straits to Cephalonia, and eastward to the mountains of Arkania in Greece.

PASSING THROUGH A WOODED GORGE.

IT IS UNDER THESE TREES THAT ULYSSES IS SUPPOSED TO HAVE LAIN WHEN THE PHAEACIANS LANDED HIM ON THE SHORES OF ITHACA.

In fact, the island of Ithaca is so narrow that at any height the sea may be seen on both sides of it; and this is one of its most picturesque attributes.

After a while we turned back, and driving down again to the east shore we struck another road, which carried us over the central mountain-ridge to a high cornice road running along the west side of the island hundreds of feet above the sea. This road, which we remembered to have seen from Corfu, leads to the village of Stavro at the northern end of the island, where pretty striped rugs are made. After driving for some distance in the direction of Stavro, we stopped the carriage, and our fellow traveller and Mr. Fearn walked on ahead, while we waited for them in a grove of old olive-trees from which there was a magnificent view over the gulf of Molo and the straits of Cephalonia. The hillsides of Ithaca are thickly carpeted in the spring with perfumed clumps of blossoming sage, mixed rosy and white cistus, harebells, brown and yellow coronilla; and this fragrant *maquis* fills the whole air with sweetness, and attracts hundreds of bees, who hummed noisily about our heads as we sat in the shade of the olives.

After a while our companions returned, and we drove back to the yacht enchanted with our glimpse of Ithaca, and regretful that we could not linger here too. At 7 p.m. however steam was up and we were off for Corfu, which we reached the next morning at daylight. We had intended on our return to Corfu to take several long drives about the island, but incessant sight-seeing had tired my eyes and brain, and on the morning of our arrival, after a brief struggle, I weakly settled down to reading and letter-writing. In the afternoon we went ashore, and drove to Pelleka, a village on the west side of the island. The way leads through endless vineyards shaded by olive-trees, and though pastoral and pretty, seemed rather monotonous after the bold scenery of the other Ionian islands.

In fact to my mind Corfu, which has received the lion's share of praise because it is the most accessible of the islands, is really the least beautiful; but as I did not drive to Paleocastrizza, perhaps I am not a fair judge.

Pelleka is a poor village on a hill, and from the olive-grove on the height above it there is a magnificent view over the outspread wooded island and the sea; but of course we were told on our return that to appreciate Corfu one must see Paleocastrizza.

The next day, to our great regret, the American Minister left us to go back to Athens, and we intended to start at 12 o'clock for Cattaro in Dalmatia; but a violent north-west gale kept us prisoners at Corfu. The sea ran so high that we could not use any of the yacht's boats to go ashore in, and even in a large Corfu boat we were drenched and very nearly swamped. However, it was one of those days when life on a yacht is unendurable, and go ashore one must at any cost, so we wandered about the town all day long, as it was too windy and dusty to drive.

The wind was still blowing hard when we woke on the following day, but as it was the Greek Palm Sunday, the great annual festival of Corfu, we were all rather glad of the excuse to stay and see the procession, in which the body of St. Spiridion, a Cypriote bishop of the fourth century, and patron of Corfu, is carried through the town.

When we went ashore we found the streets crowded with peasants in holiday dress. The King and Queen and their children, who had come by yacht from Corinth two days before, were all assembled on the balcony of the Royal Palace overlooking the Esplanade, and the scene was altogether as gay and pretty as possible. The peasant-women vied with each other in gorgeousness. Their lace *chemisettes* were covered with gold necklaces, charms, and amulets, and crosses set with pearls, and their hands were laden with rings, while on their shoes they wore enormous silver buckles—so large in fact that the English ladies in Corfu buy them, have them straightened, and use them as photograph frames. Some of the women had on finely-plaited petticoats of shot silk, white muslin aprons tied with bright ribbons, and purple velvet jackets embroidered in gold; while others were dressed in aprons of flowered brocade shot with gold and silver, over dark blue silk petticoats edged with ruffles of red and yellow silk, and all wore enormous coils of false hair twisted with red ribbons, and over their heads a drapery of white silk, a flowered kerchief, or a white lace veil draped up on the side by a wreath of artificial blossoms mixed with sprays of gold and silver flowers set high on quivering stems. Nothing, in short, can be conceived more brilliant than these groups of women wandering about under the flowering acacias on the Esplanade or standing in throngs beneath the Royal balcony.

We went at once to Mr. Woodley's house overlooking the quay, and soon afterwards the procession appeared. First came a military band, followed by men in blue cotton gowns, carrying large gilt lanterns and silk banners surmounted by silver crucifixes wreathed in flowers; these men were flanked on either side by others carrying tapers, and these again by a single file of soldiers. Then came another band, then more men carrying gigantic candles, as big as tree-trunks, and decorated with gold tinsel and flowers. These candles were fitted into leather sockets strapped over the men's shoulders, and were almost more than they could carry.

Next came a priest in black, carrying a gilt cross, and escorted by two men with tall silver candlesticks; then a procession of forty or fifty priests, marching in couples and arrayed in vestments of brocade or of brilliant blue, green or purple silk, with ornaments of gold. They walked along with folded hands, intoning a kind of chant, and after them came the Archbishop, his vestments stiff with gold, his velvet mitre covered with gold arabesques and enameled miniatures of saints, and the silver-gilt patritza in his hand. He was followed by four priests, in flowered brocade vestments, carrying a crimson canopy fringed with gold, and under this, borne also by priests, came the curious upright casket of red velvet covered with gold, which contains the body of St. Spiridion. A priest in crimson velvet starred with gold and a group of officers in uniform closed the procession.

When it had passed, and the crowd had poured after it, we left Mr. Woodley's and went to the St. George Hotel on the Esplanade, in order to get another view of the pageant on its return. From here the sight was even more beautiful. . . . Never shall I forget the brilliance of the scene as the procession came down towards the Esplanade through the marble arch on the left of the Royal Palace, the splendid colours of vestments and banners relieved against the bright blue sea and the range of Albanian mountains, and under the green boughs in the foreground, the swaying crowd of gaily dressed peasants bending the knee before their Saint's approach.

It is my latest and loveliest recollection of Corfu; for the next morning at 4 o'clock we were off for Dalmatia, and the last part of our cruise had begun.

A GROVE OF OLD OLIVE TREES.

WE WERE ENCHANTED WITH OUR GLIMPSE OF ITHACA, AND REGRETFUL THAT WE COULD NOT LINGER.

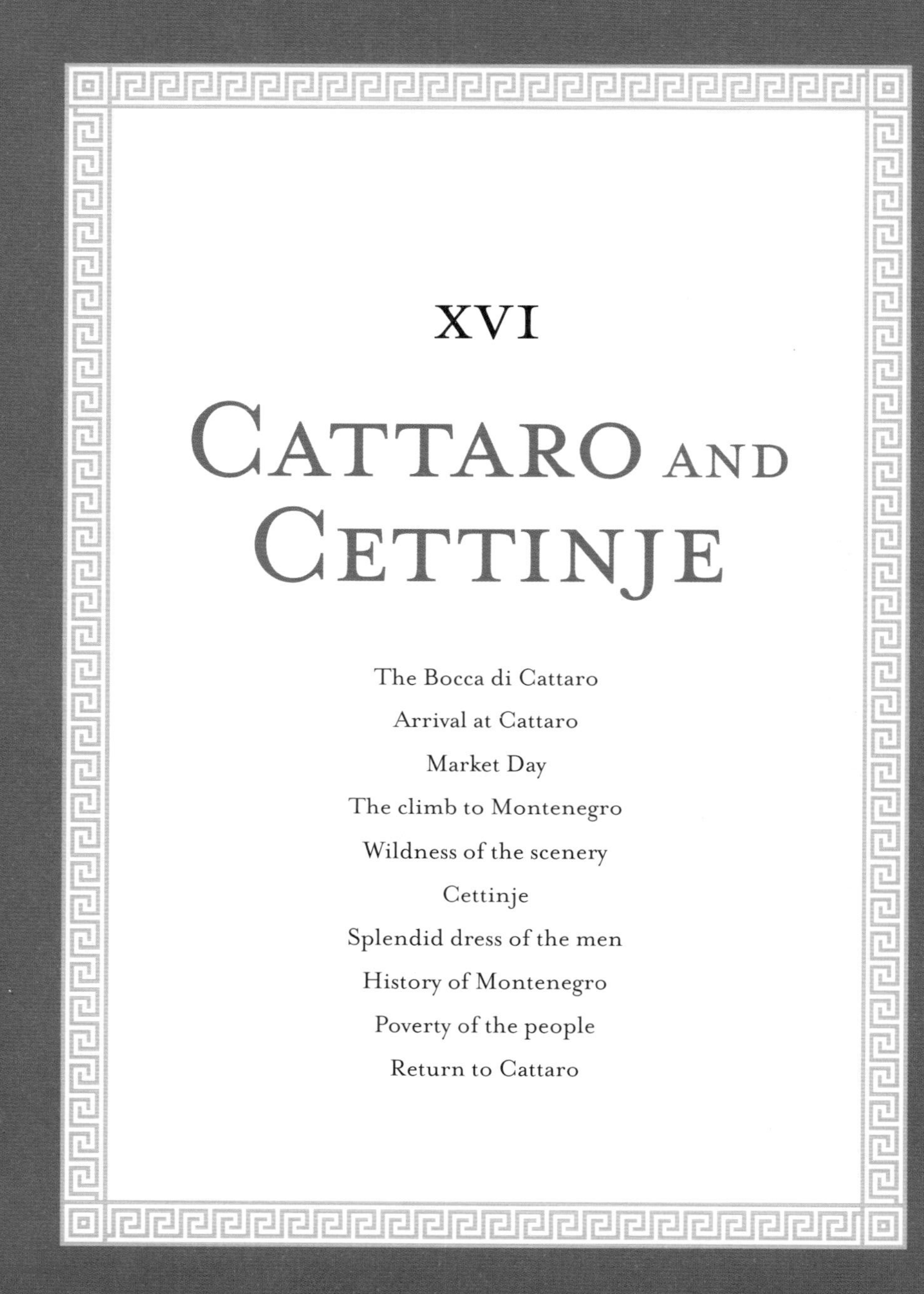

XVI

Cattaro and Cettinje

The Bocca di Cattaro

Arrival at Cattaro

Market Day

The climb to Montenegro

Wildness of the scenery

Cettinje

Splendid dress of the men

History of Montenegro

Poverty of the people

Return to Cattaro

That day as we steamed along the Albanian coast under the snow-covered mountains of northern Albania, it seemed to me that the water gradually shifted from cobalt to the misty Prussian blue of more northern seas. The "purple East" was behind us, and the Mediteranean seemed unwilling to let a drop of its lapis hue run into the Adriatic waves.

At midnight we reached the entrance of the Bocche di Cattaro, as the long, winding gulf which leads up to Cattaro is called, and anchored in a bay near Castelnuovo.

The next morning (the first of May) we were up early, and at 7 a.m. we started to steam up the gulf. It is less like an arm of the sea than a river bounded by wrinkled grey mountains, with a fringe of lovely verdure along the shore. Here and there lie white villages on the water's edge, in groves of beech and acacia.

The houses in these villages are square and ugly, but always in their midst rises a slender campanile with arcaded upper story and pointed roof.

We crossed the wide bay of Teodo, and passing through the *Catene*, the narrowest part of the gulf, we saw ahead of us, at the mountain's base, the beautiful village of Perasto, with its two sentinel islands lying before it on the glassy waters—one just large enough to hold a small Catholic chapel, the other a little Greek church with green-domed apse and belfry. Perasto itself is framed in masses of foliage, from the midst of which rise two arcaded campaniles of graceful design.

We steamed on into the bay of Risano, enclosed in mountains, with the village of Risano in an oasis of green at its head; then we turned around and, passing Perasto again, we steamed up the innermost bend of the gulf, and anchored at the quay of Cattaro. A more beautiful spot I never saw. The mountains rise on every side in the wildest magnificence, except at the very head of the gulf, where a wooded valley stretches up between them.

Cattaro itself lies at the foot of the mountains with its houses crowded in between a towering cliff crowned by an old fortress, and the calm waters of the gulf.

The whole of the cliff, from the town below to the citadel above, is walled in, and the town itself is enclosed in high walls overgrown with ivy. The quay outside the walls, shaded by beautiful trees, is the busiest spot in Cattaro. A market was being held there when we arrived, and it was crowded with Montenegrins whose handsome dresses were brightly relieved against the grey walls and green foliage.

Close behind the fortified cliff of Cattaro rise the almost perpendicular mountains, and up their face we could trace from the yacht's deck the dizzy zig-zag of the old path to Montenegro, the famous "Scala di Montenegro."

We went ashore, and passing through the picturesque market, entered the gate and took a hurried walk through the town, which deserves far more time than we could give it. The narrow streets are full of beautifully sculptured doors and windows, the inevitable traces of Venetian occupation, and there is a charming little church at which we could just glance; while here and there the dark recesses of an arched shop are gaily lit up by rows of Montenegrin dresses, embroidered coats and jackets and jaunty scarlet caps—for the Montenegrins do not do their own tailoring, but have their clothes made at Cattaro or Scutari d'Albania.

We were much tempted to linger in Cattaro, which like the other Dalmatian towns is a treasure-house of Venetian domestic architecture, but I was so anxious to go to Montenegro that my companions yielded to my entreaties and we set out at once to hire a carriage and make arrangements for the expedition.

The carriage was soon found, and at 12 o'clock we started for Cettinje, the capital of Montenegro. As far as we could see the new Austrian road from the quay it seemed to wind up pleasantly through the shady valley at the head of the gulf and lose itself around the shoulder of the mountain beyond; but after we had mounted for some distance we looked up and saw the road zig-zagging high overhead up the sheer side of the mountain-wall behind Cattaro. This was more than we, with our unsteady heads, had bargained for, but it was too late to turn back, so on we went—climbing, climbing, climbing—with always more climbing ahead of us, and the depths below growing more dreadful at each turn. We had been told by the English Consul at Corfu, who had taken the drive many times, that it would take us six hours to get to Cettinje and four to return—but we soon found that this was another of the delusive statements which are always leading poor travellers astray, for although we had fast horses it took us nearly eight hours to reach Cettinje.

After a climb of nearly four hours we reached the highest point of the road, and drove along a sort of cornice, overhanging the "Bocche" thousands of feet below. Luckily there is a parapet almost all the way, otherwise we should inevitably have jumped over the precipice, for the height is terribly dizzy. It was a beautiful day, and we could see almost the whole of the Bocche, coiled serpent-like between the mountains from Cattaro to the sea, while far, far down just under us lay the *Vanadis* like a black speck on the bay of Cattaro.

A few minutes later we crossed a diagonal line of stones in the road, and found ourselves at last in "unconquered Montenegro;" shortly after which a turn carried us out of sight of the Bocche, and after driving for a little distance between masses of grey rock, we stopped at a sort of half-way house, just four and a quarter hours after leaving Cattaro. The house was a mere stone hovel, with a round stone table in front, where we were regaled with black bread and wine by two women who spoke a few words of Italian or German, I forget which.

After half an hour's rest we started again, and drove across a wide, stony valley enclosed in rocky walls, and unshaded by a single tree. Here and there little patches of carefully cultivated wheat or vegetables appeared in the hollows of the rock, but these were the only signs of verdure. All along the road we met strings of Montenegrins, the women carrying heavy loads on their backs and heads, or driving sheep and mules, while the men strolled on ahead, lazily smoking. Wherever the road made a detour they scrambled up and down the face of the rocks like goats, and in fact it is no uncommon thing to see a Montenegrin woman knitting as she walks down the side of a sheer cliff with a great bundle balanced on her head. The people we met on the road were mostly of the poorer class, and their dresses, although picturesque, were shabby and ragged, especially those of the women who, being the drudges of the community, are seldom as gaily dressed as the men. The latter all carry black woolen plaids, with a long fringe, thrown over their shoulders; and we saw the women weaving these plaids in the doors of the houses that we passed. The women themselves carry their loads in a kind of saddle-bag of coarse woolen stuff hung with tufts of fringe, and some of them wear aprons of the same material. These bags and aprons, in varying colours and designs, are common to all the Illyrian peasants.

At the end of the valley we drove through the miserable village of Negush, the birthplace of the present princely family, a collection of stone hovels with thatched roofs. On the hills above it the light green foliage of a grove of dwarf beeches contrasted pleasantly with the universal glare of grey stone. Beyond Negush the road mounts the face of another mountain, and the snow lay in patches on the peaks above us. At last we reached the top of this final barrier, and the next turn brought us out upon one of the wildest scenes I have ever beheld.

As far as the eye can reach on every side, range after range of stony hills and valleys roll away like a stormy sea with waves of grey stone, bounded at the southern horizon by the blue lake of Scutari and the snow mountains of Northern Albania. We drove down by interminable windings, each turn bringing into view fresh wildness of stone. Here and there a few dwarf beeches fringed the road with a feathering of pale green, and in their shade grew cowslips, violets, and a little blue anemone; but these patches of vegetation grew rarer as we drove on.

We began to watch anxiously for Cettinje, for the sun was setting and the air growing very cold; but though the high peak of Lövchen rose ahead of us with the tomb of the Prince-Bishop Peter on its top, not a sign of the town could we behold. At last we turned a projecting angle of rock, and far below us at the end of a long bare plain enclosed in mountains lay a cluster of red-tiled roofs.

"Ecco Cettinje!" said the coachman; but though in sight it still seemed hopelessly far off, and although we descended rapidly and drove at a good pace across the darkening plain it was 7.30 when we reached the inn at the end of a straight road lined with low stone houses.

This road, which is the main street of Cettinje, was full of Montenegrin men in splendid dresses, who all touched their caps to us as we passed; they never uncover except to their Prince. At the inn-door we were received by our host, a tall man in a handsome dark green dress with the gold embroidered outer jacket which is the most expensive item of the Montenegrin costume. We passed through a hall, catching a glimpse of a billiard-room full of men, and were shown upstairs to our rooms. It was lucky that it was dark on our first introduction to them, for by day they were really appalling; and yet the inn of Cettinje offers such inducements of luxury to the Montenegrins that nearly all the chief men of the principality live there in preference to their private hovels. Dirty as it was I must admit that we had a very comfortable and nicely-served dinner in the large dining-room, at a table decorated with oranges and a bunch of narcissus. After dinner we presented our letters to the Hon. Walter Baring, English Chargé d'Affaires, who lives in a wretched little house opposite the hotel; then we went to bed, too tired, luckily, to look very closely into the state of our sheets and mattresses.

The next morning we were up and dressed early, and started out for a stroll. We walked through the dreary street, and saw a market where a crowd of tattered women were bargaining for a few fragments of horrid-looking food.

The poverty of Montenegro is terrible, and there is something desolate in the aspect of a town, no matter how small, which does not boast a single shop, café, garden, or place of amusement. Almost all the house-doors stood open, and as we passed down the street we looked into squalid, smoke-blackened dens where wretched women sat crouching over their work on the floor. Then we went to look at the Prince's Palace, which stands near the inn. It is a stone building painted a yellowish-green and standing in a walled garden; a sentry paces up and down before the door, and but for this the palace itself might pass for a particularly ugly New-England inn. Just near it stands the large tree surrounded by a stone bench, where the former princes of Montenegro presided over their councils; but we were told that Prince Nikita transacts all his affairs inside the Palace. Just opposite the Palace is a plain stone house with a wooden storm door, which was still more suggestive of New-England; this house is occupied by the Prince's eldest daughter and her husband, a Servian

Prince. The Prince and Princess of Montenegro always wear the national dress, and compel their subjects to do the same, even threatening them with imprisonment if they are seen in European dress. As far as I know the only individual in the principality who disregards this law with impunity is the little waiter at the inn, who was attired in a large dress suit given to him to wear as being more suitable to his calling than the national dress. The object of the law is to keep up the old national feeling; but it is very hard on the people, for the Montenegrin dress is very expensive and hard to keep clean, and the Prince will not permit any of his suite to appear with the smallest spot on their white cloth coats. The dress of the men, which is much the handsomest, consists of loose dark blue trousers, fastened at the knee with gold embroidered garters; below these are worn white cloth gaiters, knitted woolen socks, and hide shoes with interwoven white cords across the instep. The waistcoat is scarlet, richly embroidered in gold; over this is a white cloth coat, open in front, and fastened around the waist by a red woolen sash and a leather belt for arms, in which a silver-mounted pistol and yataghan are usually worn.

Then comes the sleeveless outer jacket of scarlet cloth, covered with gold and black embroidery, and edged in front with cut brass ornaments. A round scarlet cap, embroidered in gold with the national symbols, completes the costume; and the effect may be imagined of groups of tall, handsome men in this brilliant array strolling about the streets, or lounging in the door-way of the inn, which is used as a sort of club. The dress of the women is less becoming. They wear a skirt of any stuff and colour, a long sleeveless overcoat of white cloth embroidered in black and gold, and a low-necked white cloth bodice with long sleeves, fastened at the waist by a red belt embroidered in gold. Inside the bodice is a *chemisette* of striped gauze. The young girls wear a cap like the men, but with a fringed kerchief of black silk thrown over it; the married women wear the kerchief without the cap.

After the subjugation of Servia by the Turks in the fourteenth century, Montenegro asserted itself as an independent state and such it claims to have remained ever since, though in its subsequent struggles with the Turks there were doubtless moments when the might of the

Ottomans was uppermost. The capital was transferred from the lowland near Lake Scutari to the mountain-locked plain of Cettinje; but even this inaccessible stronghold has been taken and retaken by the Turks. Still, they never held it long, or were driven from it without severe loss; for in a country like Montenegro, it is hard enough for the natives to live and almost impossible for invaders.

In the fifteenth century, when Prince George abandoned Montenegro to the invasion of the Turks and fled contemptibly to end his days in ease at Venice, German the Bishop stuck to his post at Cettinje, and assumed the duties of the cowardly Prince. Thence forward the rulers of Montenegro were all ecclesiastics, either elected by the people or chosen by their predecessors, and this succession was carried on uninterruptedly until the death of the poet and reformer, the Prince-Bishop Peter II, who lies buried on the top of Lövchen. He died in 1851 and was succeeded by Danilo, who refused to enter the Church, and once more separated the offices of Prince and Bishop.

Nikita, the present ruler, was the nephew of Danilo and succeeded him in 1858.

Near the Palace stands the Monastery where the Prince-Bishops lived, and in the adjoining church Peter I and Danilo are buried. It contains no other objects of interest.

We spent the morning in front of the inn, watching the picturesque groups of men and looking at the silver pistols and yataghans which they drew from their belts, sometimes to sell, sometimes only to show us. They seemed a courteous set, and there was something touchingly incongruous in the contrast between their gorgeous fancy-ball costumes and the squalid lives they lead.

I thought they all looked bored and discontented, and no wonder, for unless they are fighting they have nothing to do, and Cettinje is not a place which offers many inducements to idleness. There are several foreign Chargés d'Affaires at Cettinje, and how they manage to live there without being driven to suicide is a mystery.

During the long winter months the town is buried in snow, in summer the sun beats down cruelly upon its unprotected street and fields.

The houses occupied by the diplomats are not fit for civilized people to live in; there are no walks, rides, or drives, if one excepts the two roads descending to Cattaro and Lake Scutari; there are no books, or papers, and the only social possibilities lie in an occasional evening spent at the Palace. These things being taken into account, it must be admitted that Cettinje cannot be a very pleasant round in the diplomatic ladder.

At 12 o'clock we went to lunch with Mr. and Mrs. Baring, and as soon afterwards as possible we started on our long drive back to Cattaro.

The expedition, although fatiguing, is well worth making to anyone fond of scenery and costumes, and the descent on the Bocche, especially as we saw it in the sunset light, is magnificent beyond words. The drive back to Cattaro took us five and a half hours, and at dinner time we were once more on board the *Vanadis*.

THE DRIVE BACK TO CATTARO TOOK US FIVE AND A HALF HOURS, AND AT DINNER TIME WE WERE ONCE MORE ON BOARD THE VANADIS.

XVII

Dalmatia

Bay of Gravosa

Ragusa

Reception by the Mayor

Drawing in the public school

Boat-building and stone-carving by the pupils

Spalato

Palace and Mausoleum of Diocletian

The view of them hidden by scaffolding

Temple of Aesculapius, its beauty

The cruise along the coast

Fishermen in distress

Their rescue by the *Vanadis*

Arrival at Zara

Arrival at Ancona and the end of the Cruise of the *Vanadis*

t 3 o'clock the next morning we left Cattaro, and when I came on deck at 9 we were at anchor in the harbour of Gravosa, the port of Ragusa, in company with a number of Austrian men-of-war whose boats, darting across the water, made the scene almost as lively as at Malta.

The bay of Gravosa is a small, land-locked sheet of water about a mile from Ragusa. It is surrounded by somewhat barren hills, but along the edge of the water there is a belt of trees with country-houses half hidden in their midst. We landed at the quay, near which stands a great plane-tree surrounded by a stone bench, and hired a carriage to drive to Ragusa. The road runs through a wooded valley and along a ridge overhanging the sea, with glimpses on either hand of villa-gardens overflowing with a wild profusion of red and yellow roses. An occasional palm here and there testifies to the warmth of the climate, and in spite of our white umbrellas we found the sun oppressively hot. We soon drew up under a row of overarching trees at the gate of Ragusa, and leaving the carriage, crossed the drawbridge over the moat, which is now dry, and planted with oaks and poplars. Ragusa is built close upon the sea, and surrounded by battlemented walls and bastions against which the waves beat; in fact it is so shut in by fortifications that from the town itself we could hardly obtain a glimpse of the sea.

On entering the inner gate of the double walls we found ourselves at one end of the main street which leads to the piazza where the principal buildings stand. On the right is a picturesque fountain, on the left the small church of the Redeemer, with a pretty wheel-window and just beyond it the large, ungainly Franciscan church, which I recognized at once from Freeman's sketch of the Campanile. This Campanile, to my mind, is spoiled by its cupola. The street itself is well-paved and exquisitely clean, as there are few carriages inside the walls; in fact, as most of the side streets are mere lanes or in many cases flights of stone steps, it is hard to say where a carriage could be driven to if it were brought into the town. As we walked on toward the Piazza, pausing to look into shop windows, we were much struck by the clean, sunshiny look of the place, as well as by the various costumes of the peasants. The Ragusan men wear a sort of modified Montenegrin dress, with the blue trousers, gaiters and jacket, but without the long coat. Among the women, many costumes are to be seen; the prettiest being those of the Canalese district, with fluted white linen headdresses like the *cornette* of a sister of charity, blue petticoats, and linen aprons tied with gold and silver ribbons. More striking, however, are the Herzegovinian women, who wear long, sleeveless coats of dark blue cloth, fringed woolen aprons not unlike a bit of Turkey carpet, large silver buckles fastening their bodices, and little red caps with white lace veils pinned over them. The main street is lined with shops where these dresses are sold, together with a quantity of old Herzegovinian embroidery.

At the end of the street we came upon the piazza, with the Rector's Palace, with its incomparable arcade, and handsome but much later inner court and staircase. As a specimen of round-arched Dalmatian work, built at a time when the rest of Europe was rioting in Decorated Gothic, this Ragusan palace is of far greater interest than the neighbouring Dogana with its too florid Venetian ogees. The two buildings, however, group together very picturesquely, and it is a pity that the Cathedral, which is close at hand, is a wretched piece of seventeenth century work, utterly unworthy of such companionship.

We wandered up and down, among the steep lanes, between high houses with an occasional window or balcony which reminded us of Venice (although St. Blaise and not St. Mark guards the gates of Ragusa) but wherever we went some tantalizing wall or tower interposed itself between us and the sea, and we could only get the merest glimpse of the Island of Lacroma off the coast, with its monastery which Maximilan of Mexico turned into a palace. As to the harbour of Ragusa, it is nothing more than a small cove, with water three fathoms deep, into which only a few boats can enter, and the port of the modern *argosies* is of course at Gravosa.

After exploring the town, we sat for a while under the trees outside the gate, and then drove back at sunset to the yacht.

The next morning we left Gravosa at 4 a.m. for the Island of Curzola, which we reached at 9 o'clock.

It is a long and rather desolate-looking island with low hills overgrown by a scrub of dark trees; but the town is most picturesquely situated in the east side, its mediaeval walls and battlemented towers looking out boldly across the narrow channel at the mountainous promontory of Sabioncello in Dalmatia.

Curzola passed from Hungary to Venice in 1420, and its walls and gates are inlaid with numerous large bas-reliefs of the winged lion, while other traces of Venetian work are to be seen all through the narrow streets, or lanes rather, in the shape of beautiful trefoiled windows and carved balcony-supports projecting from the tall houses.

The pratique officer, who came on board as soon as we anchored, offered to show us the town, and on landing we were joined by the curator of the Museum, the drawing-master of the public school, and one or two other local dignitaries whose simple courtesy and pride in their little island were delightful to see.

Outside the gate, we passed a charming loggia, overlooking the harbour, with a raftered roof supported by a beautiful colonnade. Then, going under the frowning machicoulis of the gate-tower, with its guardian marble lion, we found ourselves in one of the most curious old towns I have ever seen. All the streets, many of which are steep flights of steps, lead up to the piazza at the highest point of the town, where the parish church (once a cathedral) stands. It is a beautiful little building, which the curator of the Museum attributes to the Hungarians; that is, of course, excepting the obviously late campanile and the addition behind it. Freeman on the other hand calls it Venetian, and dates its erection after 1420; but be it Hungarian or Venetian, it has one of the most interesting façades I ever saw; its chief feature being the remarkable porch with two wingless lions resting on stone corbels in a line with the lintel of the doorway. These corbels are supported on slender columns (I think engaged) thus reversing the usual order of the Romanesque porches of Southern Italy, in which crouching animals are so often seen supporting the columns which uphold the canopy of the porch. The effect produced, though perhaps not very happy, is certainly striking, but it cannot be denied that the lions thus projected into space are rather too suggestive of gigantic gargoyles.

From the piazza we were taken to see all the carved doors and windows in the town, and the countless bas-reliefs of saints, escutcheons,

&c., with which the walls of the houses are literally encrusted. Then we went to the court-yard of the Podesta's Palace, where there is a very fine bronze knocker of early Renaissance workmanship; and thence to the Museum, a dismantled chapel in which a number of traceried window-frames and bas-reliefs are collected. Our next visit was to the Palazzo Communale, where the Mayor received us; then we were taken to the public school, where the drawing-master showed us with great pride the architectural drawings and the designs for ship-building which his pupils had made. From here we went to a little garden full of roses which has been turned into a ship-yard, where the pupils execute the designs they have made, and where, in a tangle of flowers, a half-built boat was lying; beyond this is a stone-cutter's yard, and here there were several creditable bits of stone carving also done by the school children. In fact, Curzola may well be proud of her school, and it was delightful to see the pleasure which our hosts took in showing it to us.

We were very sorry to leave the little town, which is so like a toy model of a mediaeval city, with its gates, battlements and angle-towers all intact; but we were due at Spalato that evening, and we had to hurry away feeling that there was still a great deal to be seen. We brought our friends on board the yacht, where they spent a few minutes in drinking Marsala and looking over our photographs; then they went ashore, and we got underweigh for Spalato.

We had a beautiful sail along the Dalmatian coast, close under the lee of the savage grey mountains, taking the inner channel between the islands of Lesina and Brazza and the mainland, and reaching Spalato at sunset.

On the whole the approach to Spalato is disappointing, the scenery about it is bleak without being grand, and the harbour is disfigured by the long row of modern houses built along the quay. But all this was forgotten in our dismay when we discovered that the famous campanile, next to Diocletian's Palace, the crowning glory of Spalato, was covered from top to bottom with scaffolding!

The next day worse still was in store for us. In the first place, to our astonishment and indignation, we found that it was raining hard. As we had long taken it for granted that it would never rain again, our annoyance may be imagined; the more so since our cruise was to last but two days longer, and each minute was worth its weight in gold. After luncheon the rain held up, although the weather remained windy and overcast; and as soon as it stopped raining we hurried ashore.

As Macaulay's school-boy knows, the Palace of Diocletian, which the Emperor built near his birthplace when he resigned the purple, became in the seventh century the refuge of the people of Salona; and a good part of the town of Spalato is still contained inside the Palace walls.

Along the quay the water front of the Palace still stands, but its arches are defaced and partly hidden by a row of squalid shops built in front of it; and within the walls there is such a labyrinth of houses that it is almost impossible to trace the plan of the Palace. We found our way to the court where the Mausoleum of Diocletian and the temple of Aesculapius stand, but here the greatest blow of all awaited us, for we found that the Mausoleum (which is now the Duomo) was as completely enclosed in scaffolding as the Campanile. Under these circumstances it must be confessed that Spalato is a failure. Inside the Duomo the circular form of the Mausoleum has been preserved intact, but the capitals and entablature of the lower order of columns have been entirely restored in white plaster, which contrasts cruelly with the soft tones of the sculptured frieze above.

On one side is a fine marble pulpit, with elaborately foliaged capitals, which seemed to me almost worthy to claim kinship with the Easter candelabrum of the Capella Palatina, although Murray dates it two hundred years later. I wonder if this is a mistake, or if the decidedly Romanesque character of the work is only another proof of the strange survival of Romanesque forms in Dalmatia long after they had fallen into disuse elsewhere.

The small temple of Aesculapius on the other side of the court is in a wonderful state of preservation. The columns of the porch are gone, but the exquisite mouldings of the doorway are intact, as well as the sculptured caissons of the vault, and the gorgeous but oppressive cornice below it.

As to the famous arcade which surrounds the court, where the world was first shown the true relation between the column and the arch, it would be impossible to overstate its beauty, even as it now stands with mean houses built in the inter-columniations.

From here we found our way with some difficulty to the Golden Gate, the principal entrance of the Palace. To my mind it has been somewhat overpraised. There is a meaningless look about the row of columns (now half broken away) dividing the niches above the doorway, although one may trace in them a faint suggestion of the coming arcades of Zara and Lucca, not yet reasoned out or properly applied. Very curious, too, is the useless architrave of the doorway, with a gold, round arch springing above it.

From the Golden Gate we went to the Museum, where there are some well-preserved sarcophagi; but I was more interested in looking through Adam's beautiful book, *The Ruins of Spalato*, published in 1762, of which there is a copy in the Museum.

In the course of our wanderings we walked all through that part of the town which is contained inside the walls, getting many picturesque glimpses of corbelled balconies, Venetian windows, and bas-reliefs and escutcheons built into the houses.

Here and there, too, we came upon a fragment of Roman work—Corinthian column or cornice—encrusted in the wall of a house, side by side, perhaps, with a bit of mediaeval sculpture.

The people are less picturesque than in the other Dalmatian towns, and one feels the fatal nearness of the railway. The women wear the usual sleeveless coat of dark blue cloth, curious embroidered socks, red turbans with white linen kerchiefs thrown over them, and bright woolen aprons, while the men are dressed in baggy blue trousers, red sashes full of knives and pistols, and red turbans, which give them a somewhat Oriental look.

It was a great disappointment to us not to go to Traü, which is only a few miles off, and one of the most interesting towns in Dalmatia, but the short time that was left us made it necessary to hurry on to Zara the next morning.

We had intended to leave Spalato at dawn, but the Bora blew with such violence that the pilot whom we had taken on board for our Adriatic cruise would not start until 9 a.m. We ran up the coast as close as possible under the lee of the land, and the force of the gale seemed to have flattened the sea, for the *Vanadis* went on her course quite steadily.

A short time before passing Sebenico, we were signaled by two fishing-boats in distress which were being blown out to sea. One was a sloop with several men on board, the other only a little sail-boat with one occupant. We steamed out to their rescue, and lay to while they were being tied to the yacht's stern; then the Captain gave the order "half speed" instead of "dead slow," and the yacht started ahead, giving such a jerk to the towing rope between the two boats that it broke, and the little sail-boat immediately capsized. We were off an unsheltered part of the coast, without any islands to break the strength of the gale, and a tremendous sea was running; the accident, however, would not have happened if the man in the sail-boat had not tied the rope to his mast instead of fastening it at the bow. We lay to again, and the cutter was lowered in an instant, while we all stood on deck anxiously watching the poor man who was clinging to his overturned boat, his head disappearing now and then under the great waves. Although our men pulled splendidly, the man sank under the boat twice before they reached him and lifted him safely into the cutter, and a moment later he would probably have been drowned. We steamed back to pick them up, and our men, after putting a rope from the sloop to the disabled boat, brought the man on board and gave him some brandy and warmed him at the galley-fire. Meantime we steamed ahead dead slow and made for a small port on the Dalmatian coast where we released the boats and set the poor shipwrecked man ashore. We gave him some money and a suit of clothes, and the men contributed various old coats and trousers as well, so that I think he left the *Vanadis* rather well-pleased with his adventure.

The episode was less satisfactory to us, as it delayed us over an hour, and it was sunset when we reached Zara, a beautiful little town built on a flat tongue of land with water surrounding it on three sides.

The *Vanadis* was moored to the quay in the fine harbour to the north of the town, and we hurried ashore to take a short walk before dark. Like nearly all the Dalmatian towns, Zara is enclosed in fine mediaeval walls, pierced at intervals by gates surmounted by the winged lion, and on the top of these walls an Esplanade has been laid out shaded by large trees, which is the favourite evening walk of the Zariotes.

As we wandered through the narrow streets of the town we met many peasants in holiday dress, the men in short blue jackets trimmed with red silk tassels, their waistcoats fastened with a double row of silver buttons. As to the women, they wear the usual Illyrian dress, with sleeveless coat and carpet-like apron.

We had great difficulty in finding the Duomo, as its campanile is unfinished and it is quite hidden by the surrounding houses. It was built in the 13th century and has a charming Romanesque façade, with three rows of round-arched wall-arcades pierced by two wheel-windows, one just over the other.

Unluckily it was closed, so after attempting in vain to see the ancient church of St. Donatus, which is quite shut in by houses, and garden-walls, we went on to St. Chrysogonus. This church, although built nearly two hundred years later than the Duomo, has a beautiful façade of the same character, while within it is a perfect basilica, with flat room and round arches supported on alternating piers and pillars, above which the bare wall space seems to cry for the mosaics of Monreale and Ravenna. The altars were brightly lighted and the church crowded with people, so after standing a few minutes in the doorway we went back through the darkening streets to the yacht.

We hardly liked to think, as we went on board, of all that we had left unseen at Zara, where we had intended to spend two days instead of one night; still less did we care to remember that within twenty four hours our cruise was to come to an end.

The next morning, the 7th of May, we started at 4 o'clock for Ancona, where we were to leave the yacht. The wind had dropped, but there was a heavy sea, and we rolled most uncomfortably as we crossed the Adriatic; besides which the pilot made his land fall too far to the south, and it did not add to our enjoyment to have to steam for twelve miles up the coast of Italy in face of a head sea.

At length, however, we came in view of a town nobly guarded by two commanding heights, one crowned by a fortress, the other by a church. "This is Ancona, yonder is the sea," and the cruise of the *Vanadis* has come to an end.

We anchored off the old mole, near the arch of Trajan, and five minutes later a fishing-boat drifted against us and tore her mainsail to pieces on our bowsprit. This time however, as we were securely at anchor, we did not feel responsible for the calamity.

We went ashore at once to make arrangements for taking the afternoon train to Rimini, and when we returned to the yacht all hands were mustered on the forward deck to bid us goodbye. Our fellow traveller made them a little speech, telling them how much pleased we were with their conduct during the cruise, and what pleasure we should take in reporting the fact to the owner of the *Vanadis*. He then added that we had left a cheque with the mate to be cashed and distributed among the men when the yacht reached England, and a chorus of "Thank you, Sir! Thank you, Ma'am! A pleasant journey to you!" responded to his closing words.

The baggage and servants were then sent off in the cutter to the Custom House, while we went below to dine for the last time in the cosey saloon, and I think we all felt rather melancholy as we stepped into the gig at 6 o'clock and rowed away from the *Vanadis*, pursued by a burst of goodbyes and a waving of hats and handkerchiefs from all on board.

The cruise, from first to last, was a success. The *Vanadis* proved herself a most comfortable and sea-worthy boat, and had her bottom been in proper order when she left England we should have made eleven knots an hour during the whole voyage.

As for all hands on board, with the sole exception of the Captain, who was surly and inefficient, they gave us entire satisfaction and it would be hard to find anywhere a nicer or more willing set of men.

I felt as if I were parting with old friends when I saw the last of their pleasant faces and I am glad to think, in looking back on the three months we spent together, that they liked us as much as we liked them.

THE END

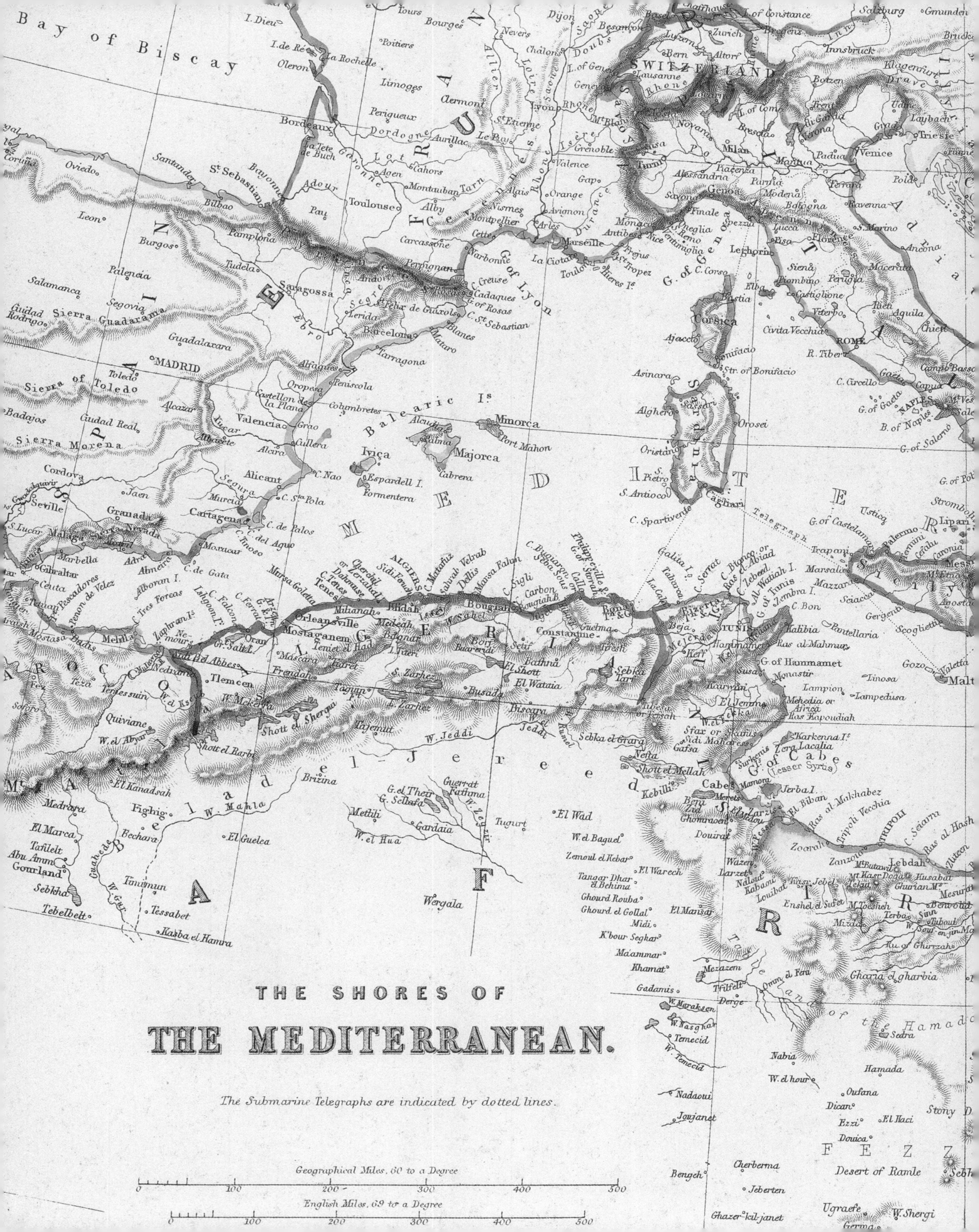
THE SHORES OF
THE MEDITERRANEAN.
The Submarine Telegraphs are indicated by dotted lines.
Geographical Miles, 60 to a Degree
0 100 200 300 400 500
English Miles, 69 to a Degree
0 100 200 300 400 500
Bay of Biscay
SWITZERLAND
G. of Lyon
G. of Genoa
Balearic Is.
Minorca
Majorca
Iviça
Corsica
Sardinia
Sicily
MADRID
Toledo
Sierra of Toledo
Sierra Morena
Sierra Guadarama
Barcelona
Valencia
Cartagena
Granada
Seville
Cordova
Gibraltar
Marseille
Toulouse
Bordeaux
Bayonne
Lyon
Milan
Venice
Genoa
Leghorn
ROME
NAPLES
Palermo
Trapani
Valetta
ALGIERS
Oran
Constantine
Bona
TUNIS
TRIPOLI
G. of Cabes
(Lesser Syrtis)
G. of Hammamet
Telegraph
Desert of Ramle
Shott el Shergui
Shott el Mellah
W. Jeddi